# ABANDON SHIP?

# ABANDON SHIP?

## TY GIBSON

**Pacific Press Publishing Association**
Nampa, Idaho
Oshawa, Ontario, Canada

**Library of Congress Cataloging-in-Publication Data**
Gibson, Ty, 1963-
    Abandon ship? : one man's struggle to discover God's special
purpose for his church / Ty Forrest Gibson.
        p.   cm.
    ISBN 0-8163-1364-4 (paper : alk. paper)
    1. Seventh-Day Adventists–Membership. 2. Commitment
to the church. 3. Church Membership.    I. Title.
BX6154.G47 1997
286.7'32—dc21

                                  96-29603
                                     CIP

# *Contents*

# *Foreword*

Each year I receive numerous requests to write forewords for books. I am able to read only a select few of the manuscripts that come to me. The constraints of my schedule necessitate that I focus on the *It Is Written* ministry. I have instructed my secretary to return any unsolicited manuscripts. As manuscripts come into the office, my secretary tells me what they are before she returns them. When we received *Abandon Ship?* by my friend, Ty Gibson, I told her to hold it for a few weeks until I could get to it. Recently, as I flew to an appointment, I picked up Ty's manuscript and could not put it down.

Ty has the ability to write interestingly as well as convincingly. He has something to say, and he says it well. As an evangelist passionately committed to preaching the gospel, in this generation, to the world in this generation, I have been concerned, concerned about our church, concerned with the fragmentation, concerned with the conflict between liberals and conservatives. While we kick theological footballs back and forth, a world is lost. People who do not know Jesus Christ are going down to Christless graves. At times we seem to be preoccupied, concerned with arguing among ourselves regarding issues that have little significance to people who are lost. There are ministries among us who claim to be predominantly revival ministries, but spend the majority of their time criticizing church administration rather than reaching out to lost people to win them for Christ. There are groups among us who will attempt to downplay the uniqueness of the Adventist message for this generation.

In his book, *Abandon Ship?*, Ty speaks directly to the fragmentation of Adventism today. He makes two significant points. First, that God desires through His church to reveal a final and full display of His love, and second, rather than a calling out to accomplish renewal, there will be a shaking out to accomplish purification. In other words, Ty's point, for which he provides strong biblical support, is that in past generations God has called out His faithful few. In this generation the worldly elements will be shaken out, and God will have a church that does reflect His love before the universe.

You'll find there is some new material here in *Abandon Ship?*; insights that are fresh from both the Bible and the Spirit of Prophecy, that speaks to the triumph of God's cause. I am a stronger, more committed Seventh-day Adventist Christian, because I have read this book. I believe that as you read it, as you go through these pages, your heart will be touched. You will be drawn to the Master, and God will broaden your vision.

It is my prayer, that, as you read these pages, you will develop greater confidence in the integrity of God's message for these last days, greater confidence in His church, and that that confidence will lead you to a renewed commitment to mission and dedication to service.

Mark Finley
SPEAKER/DIRECTOR OF *"IT IS WRITTEN"* TELECAST

# An Opening Word

For the first time in its history, the Seventh-day Adventist Church is now faced with the serious threat of fragmentation into several independently governed bodies. Such is the fate that has befallen virtually every other Protestant denomination before us. Through the process of theological debate and social divergence, Christianity has divided into countless liberal and conservative factions. Seventh-day Adventism is the only major Protestant body that still enjoys the benefits of governance under a single structure. We have prided ourselves on the fact that we are one people, under one system of order, free from the confusion and weakness of congregationalism. There have been a few stray offshoots in our history, such as the SDA Reform movement and the Shepherd's Rod. But they have done little more than position themselves at the edges of Adventism. Most people in the world and even in the church have never heard of them.

To remain *one church* has been crucial to our basic sense of identity as the remnant of Revelation. Believing ourselves to be a divinely called people with a special mission, we have referred to Adventism as a *movement of destiny.* We are the church whose task it is to take the everlasting gospel, in the light of the three angels messages, to every nation, people and language of earth. Fragmentation into more than one movement has been perceived as diametrically opposed to the preservation of this identity and the accomplishment of our mission.

Nevertheless, much to the dismay of many church leaders and members, recent decades have given rise to numerous independent ministries, both liberal and conservative, who have mustered enough boldness to venture out on their own to practice their individual versions of the Adventist faith. While most of these groups, at present, represent themselves as ministries assisting the church (whether the church appreciates their assistance or not), some have gone so far as to announce that the big boat is sinking and are urging its passengers to *Abandon Ship,* to join a new true church. Independently of the organized Seventh-day Adventist Church, and yet under claim to that name or some variation of it, ministers have been ordained, churches have been established and dedicated, tithe-receiving treasuries have been set up and missionaries have been sent out.

I personally attended a meeting in which over fifty representatives from independent groups convened to discuss how far the independence should be taken.

One speaker suggested that the denomination was in such irreparable apostasy that the courageous and faithful must consider it their responsibility to go ahead and finish the gospel commission without the organized church. Another agreed and said it was a matter of religious duty that the independent ministries collect tithe money so as to prevent its misuse by the denomination and to insure that it be devoted to finishing the work. At this point, all but a few voices were offering hearty amens to support the adventurous agenda.

Then another prominent leader from a well-known independent ministry arose to speak. His presentation was serious and commanded the attention of all present. As he developed his line of reasoning a heavy silence hung over the room. His suggestions seemed to be the logical conclusion to what had been presented by the other speakers.

"It's time to organize local churches," he explained with a tone of authority. "We need to set up conferences and select leadership to guide the world-wide work."

A weak rumble of agreement passed through the room. As the proposal gained momentum, other leading voices, the same voices that had urged the independent agenda up to this point, began to ardently disagree with going so far as to openly start a new denomination. I'll never forget the point that was made next.

"Listen," the retort came, "for all practical purposes, we have already started a new church, just short of openly admitting it. We have our own missionaries, our own preachers, our own periodicals, our own treasuries, our own leaders, our own camp meetings and church services. Beyond all this, we believe that the organized church is in apostasy. Why are we afraid to follow through and get organized as a church?"

Good point!

No good answer.

These are the kind of discussions that are taking place on the edges of Adventism at the conservative end of the spectrum. And similar issues are pending at the liberal end of the spectrum as well. There is at least one celebration-style church that has taken the big step to declare itself an independent Adventist congregation. At the 1995 Utrecht General Conference session, there was talk of local congregations and conferences ignoring the world church's vote against woman's ordination. Bold independence is mounting. The sense of need to remain one cohesive body is weakening as Adventism ages.

Will the Seventh-day Adventist Church be able to remain a single-mission-driven body of believers? Or will the denomination eventually break up into a variety of separate mini-movements? Is the church in apostasy? Is it time to abandon ship? Serious divisions do seem inevitable at this point, but perhaps we should ask another question:

What is God's plan? How does the divine agenda read?

Whatever we may think about the future of the church, there is One who "worketh all things after the counsel of His own will" (Ephesians 1:11). Certainly, the prophetic mission of Revelation's remnant church will be accomplished by someone, somehow, sometime. Having that confidence, it would be wise for each of us to discover the divine will through an earnest and prayerful study of the Bible and the Spirit of Prophecy.

I am of the conviction that the Lord has made Himself clear in the inspired revelations of His Word and the modern manifestation of the gift of prophecy. These sources of divine wisdom open to our understanding the mystery of God's will and answer every vital question.

Whom on earth does God recognize as His church?

What is the Lord's ultimate purpose for His church?

Is God leading out independent movements to accomplish His will?

How will the Lord separate the faithful and the unfaithful?

Is Adventism as we know it destined for failure or triumph?

How can I make sure I'm a part of whatever God has planned?

There is no need to venture a guess to any of these questions. The inspired answer to each one is unmistakably clear.

I don't want to pretend that everyone who reads this book will find total resolve regarding this crucial topic, but I offer what my study of the inspired counsel and my personal experience have taught me concerning God's plan for His church. For me, the insights set forth in the following pages have, indeed, brought sweet resolve after years of intense wrestling with the issue. I can't help but hope that firm conclusions will be reached by some as they read this book. Like me, they have struggled over the matter long enough. It's time for the picture to come clear at last. For others, I simply pray that what I have written here will sufficiently agitate the matter to prompt a more energetic quest for understanding.

# CHAPTER ONE
# *A Rude Awakening*

It was March of 1982. My beautiful new bride and I were baptized in the name of the Father and of the Son and of the Holy Spirit. What a glorious day it was! Not only were we now Christians—that would have been wonderful enough—but we were members of *the* one and only "remnant church" of Bible prophecy. Somehow, no doubt by God's tender mercy, we passed through the winding maze of this world's religious confusion straight into the Lord's end-time movement.

What an undeserved privilege!

What an awesome calling!

And little did I know, what an intense battle!

In a matter of just a few short months I found my newborn-self standing saucer-eyed and baffle-brained in the midst of a spiritual war zone whose weapons are words and attitudes . . . and Spirit of Prophecy quotations.

17

# Abandon Ship?

Don't get me wrong. I wasn't *totally* naive. Sure, I expected some trouble, but I expected it from the world. The evangelist had told me to prepare for a few hassles from the devil. "It's the good *fight* of faith," he warned with emphasis on the word *fight*. "The devil will try to derail your new love for Christ."

The evangelist was right.

I lost my job for the Sabbath. I lost some good friends due to the changes in my lifestyle. And I lost my mother to cancer. All in the first chapter of my Christian experience. Yeah, I'd say Satan was mad.

Fortunately, I was so high on God's love and so impressed with His Word that my trials seemed light. Even when my mother passed away I found deep peace in knowing the truth about death and the resurrection. I had so much hope and joy in my new found faith. And why shouldn't I? After all, I was now in fellowship with the saints, or at least I thought I was. Well, yeah, I was, but to my utter surprise (the evangelist said nothing about this), all in Zion were not as saintly as I had expected. In fact, some were quite unsaintly (that's a tactful way of saying they were downright mean).

I was caught off guard. Not once had I even entertained the idea of problems within the church. Come what may from the outside, I knew I was safely abiding within the borders of God's true church, surrounded by totally Christlike people who all believed and lived the very same truths I had learned in the evangelistic meetings. Nobody had even mentioned the "wheat and tares" idea. Boy, oh boy, was my cloud nine mind-set in for a rude awakening.

Before even a year had passed from the date of

my baptism, I began to realize that all was not as holy and happy in modern Israel as I had imagined. Every direction I turned presented to my young, curious gaze another issue under debate:

- In the area of theology—the nature of Christ, the nature of sin, the investigative judgment and 1844, perfection, reapplication of prophecy, feast days, Bible translations, the Spirit of Prophecy.
- With regards to standards—diet, dress, entertainment, competitive sports, jewelry, Sabbath observance.
- Concerning church government—structure, authority, women's ordination, use of tithe, lawsuits, independent ministries, health care systems.

All of these issues and others were being hotly debated when I stepped fresh from the world into the church at eighteen years of age. It should come as no surprise to any long time church member that new converts are sometimes "blown away," or should I say "tested," when they enter the ranks of Adventism. The voices in the church are many, and they're not all saying the same thing. I plead with you, please be patient with newcomers. They have much to sort out.

"Pssst," one of the voices whispered to me, "the church is in apostasy."

"The new theology (*whatever that is,* I thought to myself) is taking over," said another.

"Church leader's are mishandling God's money," was the claim of still another.

# Abandon Ship?

"In fact," the line of reasoning continued, "the true church is made up of only totally faithful people."

Needless to say, my head began to spin. So naturally, I began to ask lots of questions. And believe you me, I got lots of answers, most of which came from those who were against the church. Slowly but surely I found my heart tending away from the church. My attitude began to change toward church leaders, although I didn't realize it at first. My focus was gradually shifting from Christ and His gospel to the church and its problems. Before too long I found myself entertaining a pattern of thinking that went something like this:

"The organized Seventh-day Adventist Church is no longer the true church. It was at one time, but not any longer. The true church is composed of only faithful people who strictly keep God's commandments and follow the Spirit of Prophecy. The organized church is in apostasy, leading people into a 'new theology' and exercising an authority that does not come from God. Church leadership rejected the latter rain message in 1888, rebelled against God's plan of church organization in 1901 and sold out the truth for a weak evangelical theology in 1955 and 1956. Step by step the church has corrupted its educational, medical and theological institutions and conformed to the world.

"*Therefore* (the big conclusion), it is no longer God's church, and association with it is dangerous. The *true church* is made up of only those who are true and faithful. So I had better take my stand for the Lord before I end up deceived with the rest of the denomination."

# A Rude Awakening

The more distance I created between myself and the church, the more susceptible I became to negative reports and suspicions about the church. Finally, some of the people I found myself associating with began to suggest that the organized Seventh-day Adventist Church had become a part of Babylon.

For all practical purposes I was pretty much separated from the denomination, but somehow I still believed that it was God's church. The idea that it was Babylon seemed too bold. I could feel something driving me to that position, and yet I sensed that to take such a stand would be a daring venture away from God's will. As much as I pondered the idea, and as pushed as I felt, I never could get the words to come out of my mouth—"the church is Babylon." But the fact is, even though I couldn't take that position in an open, blatant way, my influence and example were definitely leading people in that direction. Soon this humbling reality would confront me without mercy and demand that I carefully rethink my direction.

For almost a year I could feel the issue building pressure inside my heart and mind. I was being pressed to a conclusion. One Ellen White compilation after another came my way intending to prove that the church had become Babylon. Sermon cassettes and video's on the subject piled up in my office. People I loved and respected were jumping ship with both feet.

What was I to do?

On the one hand, I had pretty much accepted the idea that the true church is composed of only the faithful and that the organized church was in apostasy. Why not take the logical next step and totally renounce the denomination and join a new movement, or start one myself for that matter?

On the other hand, I felt restrained from taking that position. All the pieces of the puzzle were not yet in place for me. Deep inside I knew the Seventh-day Adventist Church was vitally significant to God's plan, but I just was not sure how or why.

At the peak of my anxiety over the matter, a new movement arose in the church and quickly separated itself. "The Lord Our Righteousness" by name, it was made up of pastors and lay people who came to two basic conclusions: (1) Those who are truly converted are sinless, they know it, and they should declare it. (2) The organized church is Babylon and all who are truly faithful to God must separate from her communion and join the true church—"The Lord Our Righteousness."

I was so startled by this movement that I immediately began an intense study of the claims it made. Gathering together all I could find in both the Bible and the Spirit of Prophecy on the two issues raised, my conclusions were decisive and satisfying.

1. No, a truly converted person does not announce himself to be sinless or perfect, not merely because he's too humble to make such a claim, but because it simply is not the case.

2. No, the Seventh-day Adventist Church is not Babylon or any part of Babylon and never will be, nor is there ever going to be any God-inspired movement that makes such a pronouncement.

So at least that aspect of the church issue was resolved in my mind. However, I would soon discover that there was much more to the matter than simply concluding that the church is not Babylon. There were still many independent ministries and individuals who, for whatever reason, would never dare call the church Babylon, and yet, in practice and teaching, they were exerting an influence of division and separation. I associated in these circles, and quite frankly, it seemed to me that the only reason we refused to actually denounce the church as Babylon was because we knew the Spirit of Prophecy said not to. Nevertheless, the prevailing attitudes and insinuations just as surely led to separation as if we did openly declare the church Babylon.

To the satisfaction of many, one independent ministry leader would frequently (and still does) articulate the position like this:

"The church is not Babylon," he would say, assuring us of a sound Spirit of Prophecy stance, "but the church is only the true and faithful, and the organized church is in apostasy."

It's a clever play on words (I think), but such reasoning fails to commit to any definable position.

"So what exactly are you saying?" I probed on one occasion. "Are you saying that the Seventh-day Adventist Church is not Babylon, or are you saying that the true and faithful believers are not Babylon, which would leave the Seventh-day Adventist Church in question."

To which I received the answer, "No, no, the church is not Babylon, but the church is the true and faithful, and the organized church is in apostasy."

"Oh, I see," was my not so whole-hearted reply.

The fact is, I didn't see . . . at all. I was blind to

the truth about God's church, and I desperately longed for enlightenment. Praise God, the light was coming. The hour of crystallization was not too far away. Soon God would open my mind and it would all make sense. The pieces of the puzzle were accumulating to form a clear picture.

First, I was certain that the Seventh-day Adventist Church was not Babylon. There were just too many quotations that clearly denounced that idea.

Second, I could see numerous inspired statements that identified the Seventh-day Adventist Church as God's true remnant.

Third, there were other quotations that clearly pointed to a church composed of only true and faithful believers. This posed a significant problem, because there were many quotations equally as clear that identified the organized church, composed of both faithful and unfaithful members, as God's true church on earth.

Fourth, the inspired writings made it clear that there would be a time of character development, followed by a time of crisis that would cause a sifting process to occur. Out of that period of testing would emerge a body of believers composed only of wheat and no tares.

A fifth, and crucial part of the picture, presented itself as well. A reoccurring terminology was evident throughout the Spirit of Prophecy that would eventually clarify the issue. Over and over again the church was identified as having two phases of existence during its sojourn in the world. Phase One: "the church militant." Phase Two: "the church triumphant."

## A Rude Awakening

Once I understood the *church militant, church triumphant* concept, God's larger plan began to come into focus. I started to realize that the Lord intends to accomplish something grand and glorious through His church—something of universal impact and eternal magnitude.

When the light dawned upon me, I could see that the enemy of God had almost stolen from me the privilege being a part of a master plan, conceived in the infinite heart of God, to prepare a people to give the crowning revelation of His love to the world. The very church I had almost cast aside as worthless, I came to recognize as God's chosen "Theater of Grace."

CHAPTER TWO

# *Theater of Grace*

Every now and then I come across a provocatively veiled passage in the Bible or the Spirit of Prophecy that seems to say,

"Pursue my meaning. Unravel my mystery. The truth beyond will be sweet to your soul."

The words trace before my mind's eye the unfeatured silhouette of something I sense is wonderful, though not yet clear. Behind the shadowy outline apparent at first glance, I strain to see some facet of divine wisdom hidden from my comprehension. You have no doubt had the same experience in your spiritual journey.

I'll never forget an extremely hot afternoon in Australia when one such inspired quotation presented itself to my attention. I was traveling from city to city conducting revival and realignment seminars. I say revival and realignment seminar because . . . well . . . because some folks needed realignment more than revival. At almost every speaking engagement I encountered groups of estranged Adventists who were separated from the organized church and determined to oppose it. Over and over again I found myself engaged in mind-bending debates regarding whether or not the church had become Babylon.

Strongly convicted that the church was not Babylon, I was armed with all the quotations I needed to support my position. And yet . . . somehow . . . I felt like something major was missing from my understanding of the whole issue. And there was.

Sure, I was confident that the church wasn't Babylon. You've got to be deceived or deceitful to miss that point in the Spirit of Prophecy. "But why," I would ask myself in the privacy of my own grappling. "Why is it so important to stay connected with the church? So what if people want to separate and start new movements? What makes the church such a crucial component in God's plan? What does He intend to do with the church?"

Not being raised in the church, I felt no cultural loyalty to it. I knew, as well, that salvation comes through Christ alone, not by virtue of church-membership. And yet I also knew that being a part of God's visible, organized church was important. I had read statements that persuaded me of that much. But I really didn't understand why.

With numerous questions looming in my mind, I was primed to embark on a course of study that would yield a very satisfying harvest of understanding. My mind was poised for answers.

As we cruised down the kangaroo trodden highways of Australia toward Queensland, I sat in the back seat roasting in the severe heat while my Aussie host drove. We had a long journey ahead of us. As the pavement passed I fluctuated between consciousness and unconsciousness. In my lap lay a devotional book I was working my way through, one of my fingers inserted between the pages to keep my place. Each time I'd awaken, my eyes would automatically turn downward to take in a few more paragraphs before I'd pass out again.

After a few hours of this kind of uncomfortable, half-cocked reading, I laid eyes on some breath-taking words—words that quickened me with wonder and curiosity, words of startling simplicity and overwhelming depth:

"The grace of Christ must mold our entire being, and its triumph will not be complete until the heavenly universe shall witness habitual tenderness of feeling, Christlike love, and holy deeds in the deportment of the children of God" (*Amazing Grace,* p. 235).

I quickly sat up, guzzled down half a quart of water, and read the words again and again and again (you may want to do the same).

"The grace of Christ must mold our entire being. . . ." This opening line wasn't anything new to me. I had already come to understand divine grace as a transforming influence, besides being unmerited favor. But then I read on.

". . . and its triumph will not be complete until the heavenly universe shall witness. . . ." Now this was a new thought. Not only is the grace of Christ a transforming influence, but it is in the process of gaining a triumph that will extend beyond the experience of the individual sinner, a triumph that will reach beyond this world to have its effect upon the minds of heavenly intelligences. Those who inhabit the unfallen universe are focused earthward awaiting the complete triumph of God's grace.

Wow!

So what will that complete triumph look like?

". . . its triumph will not be complete until the heavenly universe shall witness habitual tenderness of feeling, Christlike love, and holy deeds in the deportment of the children of God."

You weren't expecting that anymore then I was. Surely it can't be that personal, that practical, that elementary. But, alas, it is. The whole heavenly universe—the noble and sinless angels along with the citizens of other worlds—are waiting, even longing, to see God's people relate to one another with feelings of "tenderness."

Tenderness?

Yes, that's what it says. They are waiting to see us manifest "Christlike love" toward one another. They are waiting for us to reveal "holy deeds" toward one another. Habitually—as a natural impulse springing forth from hearts that truly love like God loves!

As you can see, this inspired statement suggests some very elevated ideas. As I read it repeatedly, a glorious spiritual reality started to dawn on my mind. I began to realize that the church is, in a spiritual sense, a theater in which the power of God's grace is to be vindicated before the onlooking universe. And get this: the simple (or not so simple) matter of how we relate to one another as fellow church members is the visible testimony through which God intends to accomplish this high purpose. It's almost unthinkable, but the Lord has actually invested the future glory of His eternal kingdom in His church—in the likes of you and me.

Here is an amazing quotation that really magnifys this truth:

"From the beginning it has been God's plan that through His church shall be reflected to the world His fullness and His sufficiency. The members of the church, those whom He has called out of darkness into His marvelous light, are to show forth His glory. The church is the repository of the riches of the grace of Christ; and through the church will eventually be made manifest, even to 'the principalities and powers in heavenly places,' the final and full display of the love of God" (*The Acts of the Apostles,* p. 9).

Incredible!

Don't miss one line in this statement. God has a "plan." It's not new. It didn't just occur to Him in the last few thousand years. He's always had this plan, "from the beginning." The great purpose of the plan is to reveal the "fullness and sufficiency" of His character, to "show forth His glory," to make manifest to this world and to the unfallen universe "the final and full display" of His love. Then comes the totally amazing part of it all. It is "through the church" that the Lord "eventually" intends to accomplish this grand and glorious exploit.

Upon further study I discovered that Paul addresses this topic in detail. (It was exciting to encounter these insights in the Spirit of Prophecy, but it was truly illuminating to discover them in the Holy Scriptures.) Follow Paul's inspired reasoning

as he outlines the subject in his epistle to the
Ephesians.

In chapter one, verses four and five, the apostle
informs us that God has "chosen us in Him [Christ]
before the foundation of the world, that we should
be holy and without blame before Him in love: having predestined us unto the adoption of children by
Jesus Christ to Himself, according to the good pleasure of His will."

These words describe a pre-established divine
purpose, a pre-planned agenda for redeemed
humans. Before this world was created, no doubt
before Lucifer rebelled, divine foresight beheld the
great warfare that would arise between good and
evil. In His infinitely wise and loving heart, the
Lord devised a plan by which He would conquer
evil—a plan that would involve His heavenly son,
Jesus Christ, and His earthly children, the church.

Fallen yet redeemed human beings would be
"chosen," not for what they are in themselves, but
for what they would become *in Christ*. Through the
plan of salvation they would become "holy and without blame before Him in love." In God's chosen ones
there would be manifested a special quality of holiness that finds its reason *in love*. Not in fear. Not in
spiritual pride. Not even in a sense of duty to do
right because it is right. But wholly in love.

Holiness apart from love equates to Phari-
seeism (the Greek word for Pharisee means *separatist*). People who pursue holiness without the
actuating, softening influence of God's love end up
mad and mean. Mad at themselves for their own
failures, and mean toward others in an unconscious

effort to compensate for their personal sense of inability to measure up. The Lord is not interested in having His people merely strive to behave in outward likeness to holiness. Their is no better formula for spiritual disaster. He desires that we would truly come to love and adore Him through the influence of Calvary, and out of that experience to live holy lives for a higher purpose than to secure personal salvation. Only in the light of the cross is true holiness shaped in the believer. And it is this kind of holiness to which Paul directs our attention. He anticipates that out of the womb of love-motivated holiness something great will be born into the universe.

In the next verse Paul says that the plan God has devised will accomplish "the praise of the glory of His grace, wherein He hath made us accepted in the beloved" (verse 6). God's exercise of grace toward sinners will manifest His character with such unprecedented beauty that He will, by the triumphant virtue of that grace, win to Himself unprecedented glory and praise. By accepting sinners through Christ, and creating in them a love that manifests itself in holiness, divine grace intends to prove itself worthy of eternal adoration and loyalty.

Continuing on in Ephesians chapter one, Paul develops his theme into a truth that will impact the entire universe: "In whom we have redemption through His blood, the forgiveness of sins, according to the riches of His grace; wherein He hath abounded toward us in all wisdom and prudence; having made known unto us the mystery of His will, according to His good pleasure which He hath purposed in Himself: that in the dispensation of the fullness of times He might gather together in one all things in Christ, both which are in heaven, and which are on earth; even in Him: in whom also we have obtained an inheritance, being predestinated according to the purpose of Him who worketh all things after the counsel of His own will: that we should be to the praise of His glory, who first trusted in Christ" (Ephesians 1:7-12).

Follow Paul's reasoning:

- As a rich manifestation of His grace, God has forgiven us through the blood of Christ (verse 7).
- This response to our rebellion (the manifestation of grace) was an exercise of wisdom and prudence on God's part (verse 8).

In what sense?

- Because (here's the bottom line) the revelation of divine grace in Christ would win the eternal loyalty of the intelligent creation in both heaven and earth (verse 10).
- Redeemed humanity would become a medium of praise and glory to God by which He would secure the universal harmony of the kingdom (verse 12).

The great controversy between good and evil began with Lucifer's accusations against the character and government of God. Therefore, the manner in which the Lord deals with the rebellion is crucial. Imagine what the response of the onlooking universe may have been if God had simply obliterated man the moment he entered into league with Satan. Wisdom and prudence dictated a far more illuminating and stabilizing response. God would lovingly exercise mercy rather than immediately execute justice. Oh yes, justice would come, but only after the true character of Satan and the true character of God would be made to stand in distinct contrast. By revealing love and acceptance toward us, the Lord would win our allegiance and prove to the onlooking intelligences of heaven that He is, indeed, a God of unbounded love. By responding with grace to the sin problem, the Lord would gather to Himself the universal loyalty He is due. "All things," Paul says, referring to all intelligent, volitional creatures, "in heaven and on earth," would be united together in one kingdom of peace under Jehovah's righteous rule.

In verse 18, the apostle again emphasizes the ultimate purpose of God's plan: that we "may know what is the hope of His calling, and what the riches of the glory of His inheritance in the saints." The Lord calls us to redemption for a larger, more significant objective than to merely secure our eternal life. His calling upon sinners who are saved by grace is that we would become a channel through which He will receive a rich inheritance of glory. "In the saints," Paul says, God will inherit glory by virtue of what His grace accomplishes in them. As important as our salvation is to us and to God, the bigger picture reveals that *the way* God saves us will achieve the stability of His kingdom and the vindication of His character.

Chapter one of Ephesians concludes with an enlarged view of the saints, as one body with many members, through which the complete fullness of Christ will eventually be manifested: "And hath put all things under His feet, and gave Him to be the Head over all things to the church, which is His body, the fullness of Him that filleth all in all" (Ephesians 1:22, 23).

By virtue of His Saviorhood, Christ has gained eternal dominion over all the universe. The Father has placed everything under His reign. A special and significant relationship has been established between Christ and the church. Christ is the head. The church is His body. The head-body metaphor is intended to illustrate the vital union which is to exist between Christ and His people. The head, or mind, is the intelligent, governing power in human experience. The body is the medium through which the mind finds expression. The church is to be as a body through which Christ may reveal His own glory and accomplish His own will.

Ultimately, according to Paul, the church is to become a channel through which "the fullness" of Christ will be revealed. The Greek word for fullness (pleroma) in this text means completion in a complimentary or supplementary sense; as something that fills up or completes or supplements something else. The idea Paul intends to convey is that the church constitutes a supplementary source of glory for Christ. As its head, Christ moves in and through the church to display the complete measure of His glory.

The church has no intrinsic glory of its own by which it can offer anything to Christ for which He lacks. Of Himself Christ is the One who "filleth all in all." He is the sum total of all glory reflected in all things. He is the original source of everything praiseworthy in all things. Therefore the church is not the manufacturer of any glory by which Christ is exalted. But rather, the church is the medium through which Christ, the source of all glory, chooses to exhibit that glory. He is dependent on the church for glory by choice rather than of necessity. This truth highlights our great privilege, not His need. He has chosen us not because He needs us, but because He loves and desires us.

Looking forward to the church's eventual, triumphant standing, Ellen White penned these incredible words:

"Christ looks upon His people in their purity and perfection as the reward of all His sufferings, His humiliation, and His love, and the supplement of His glory—Christ the great center, from whom radiates all glory" (*SDA Bible Commentary,* vol. 4, p. 1180).

Could you have ever conceived of such an elevated calling for yourself and your church—to actually be Christ's "reward," His "inheritance," the "supplement of His glory." What an absolutely incredible privilege!

In chapter two Paul goes on to explain that God has exalted sinners in Christ so "that in the ages to come He might shew the exceeding riches of his kindness toward us through Christ Jesus" (verse 7). Extending far into the endless reaches of eternal ages to come, the Lord will point to the rich grace He exercised toward fallen humanity as the indisputable evidence of His goodness and love.

With concise wisdom, born of Holy Spirit inspiration, Paul goes on to lay before us the mysterious wonder of divine grace:

"For by grace are ye saved through faith; and that not of yourselves: it is the gift of God: not of works, lest any man should boast. For we are His workmanship, created in Christ Jesus unto good works, which God hath before ordained that we should walk in them" (Ephesians 2:8-10).

Here we see why the outpouring of grace is such an infinite source of glory to God. Grace is a manifestation of the divine character that truly persuades us of the Lord's worthiness to receive our highest honor, our deepest devotion, our most passionate praise.

So what exactly is this divine attribute of God's character we call *grace*?

Grace is the sublime reality of God, who is infinitely holy in all His ways; God, whose law requires perfect obedience; God, who by His mighty power could speak a word to obliterate all that now is and start creation all over again; grace is this God choosing to forgive men and women who have mocked His holiness, rebelled against His law, and denied His power.

Grace is God sacrificing His own happiness, His own comfort, His own life, to secure our happiness, our comfort, our life. Not because of obligation, but because He loves us. Not because we deserve it, but because He wants to give it. Not because we can do anything to merit it, but because His heart longs for our eternal joy.

When we see the true reality of divine grace, we see with new eyes. We see the true picture of God. We see that He is magnificently beautiful!

And once we have seen His grace, we then begin to experience its creative influence. Having been saved by grace, we then become the transparent medium through which the true glory of the Grace-full One's character is manifested. Paul says we become "His workmanship, created in Christ Jesus unto good works."

*He the Workman, we His workmanship.*
*He the Master artist, we His masterpiece.*
*He the Composer, we His symphony.*
*He the Poet, we His poiema.*

Paul is clear, we are not saved by our good works. Rather, we are saved by an excellent grace whose powerful influence creates in us a masterpiece of divine reflection. Therefore it is God, by whose grace the work is wrought, who is glorified in our salvation.

Let's back up now to my original question: What makes the church such a crucial part of God's plan?

The Lord has chosen the church—not a single individual, not many individuals scattered and separated, not small independent atoms, but a corporate body—to be the medium through which He will reveal the glory of His grace to this world and to the onlooking universe. The church is the theater in which the sufficiency of God's love to overcome evil will be demonstrated.

The following quotation brings the whole picture into focus:

# Abandon Ship?

"The church of Christ, enfeebled, defective as she may appear, is the one object on earth upon which He bestows, in a special sense, His love and His regard. The church is the theater of His grace, in which He delights in making experiment of mercy on human hearts. The Holy Spirit is His representative, and it works to effect transformations so wonderful that angels look upon them with astonishment and joy. Heaven is full of rejoicing when the members of the human family are seen to be full of compassion for one another, loving one another as Christ has loved them" (*Special Testimonies to Battle Creek Church,* pp. 18, 19).

- The church is His theater of grace.
- The Lord is using the church as an experimentation laboratory to demonstrate the transforming power of His mercy upon human hearts.
- The accomplishments of mercy are so wonderful that the angels are astonished.
- When the members of the church relate to one another with the same merciful compassion with which God has regarded them, the intelligences of heaven rejoice.

The very attribute of His character that God is most eager to reveal to the world is the one we seem the least eager to emulate in the church.

It is *tender mercy* that He longs for us to see in Him and manifest toward others.

It is *undeserved grace* by which He has saved us, and it is through eyes moist with appreciation for His grace that He desires us to look upon one another.

It is *pardoning love* that He uses to draw us away from sin to Himself, and it is with this same love that He wants us to evangelize the world.

I know now why the church is such a vital part of God's plan. I know now why He is so patient with Her failings.

It is grace. All because of grace.

# CHAPTER THREE

# God's Church Identified

Probably one of the most dangerous tendencies we possess as human beings is to draw conclusions with insufficient information. The reason this is so dangerous is because once we settle on a position and voice it to others, pride of opinion becomes a major obstacle to change, even when additional light demands it. Then, the strength of conviction that could have been fastened to the truth through adequate study is stubbornly devoted to error in order to save face.

Never have I seen this spiritual tragedy so graphically illustrated as I did in a man I'll call Brian.

When I first met Brian he seemed to be a very sincere, devoted Seventh-day Adventist Christian. Like me he was a new convert. Like me he was grappling with the church issue and trying to figure out God's will regarding the matter.

"I'm going to study the subject," he assured me. And so he did . . . somewhat.

A few months later I met up with Brian again.

"Ty, I've come to a conclusion on the church issue."

"Oh yeah; what is it?" I questioned, eager to know.

"I've found some Spirit of Prophecy statements that are so clear no one needs to be confused."

Certainly I didn't want to be confused any longer. And if there were some inspired quotations that would conclusively settle the issue, I wanted to read them.

"Share them with me, Brian."

"The first one is in *The Acts of the Apostles,* page 11. Listen: 'From the beginning, faithful souls have constituted the church on earth.' That's clear, Ty. Only faithful souls constitute God's church on earth.

"Here's another one," he continued, "and its even more clear: 'God has a church. It is not the great Cathedral, neither is it the national establishment, neither is it the various denominations; it is the people who love God and keep His commandments. . . . Where Christ is even among the humble few, this is Christ's church, for the presence of the High and Holy One who inhabiteth eternity can alone constitute a church' (*Upward Look,* p. 315)."

"Words couldn't be plainer," Brian waxed bold in his discovery. "No denomination is God's church, and that includes the Seventh-day Adventist denomination. Only those who love God and keep His law make up the true church. Case closed! That's what the Spirit of Prophecy plainly says."

And so it does. But that's not all it says, as we shall see.

In a matter of just a few months Brian had compiled all the quotations he could find that identify God's church as faithful souls. His compilation also included a chronological string of statements arranged in such a way as to prove that the Seventh-day Adventist Church had closed its probation and become Babylon. He published his findings in a book and sold thousands of copies. Soon he was traveling the globe promoting his book and calling people to separate from the organized church.

While Brian's compilation of quotations seemed conclusive to him, it wasn't for me. I had previously read many of the quotations Brian called to my attention. But I had also read other equally inspired statements that spoke of "the church" in a different way. Statements like this one:

"Although there are evils existing in the church, and will be until the end of the world, the church in these last days is to be the light of the world that is polluted and demoralized by sin. The church, enfeebled and defective, needing to be reproved, warned, and counseled, is the only object upon earth upon which Christ bestows His supreme regard" (*Testimonies to Ministers,* p. 49; emphasis supplied).

The same inspired author who penned words to portray "the church" of God as "faithful souls," also wrote that "there are evils existing in the church, and will be until the end of the world."

To simply place these quotations side by side seems to present a blatant contradiction. How could the church be composed of only faithful souls and at the same time have evils existing within her borders? With more thorough study we find perfect harmony between the two groups of statements.

# Abandon Ship?

There are two usages of the term "the church" in the Spirit of Prophecy. Sometimes Ellen White speaks of the church as every honest, faithful person on earth, of whatever nation or denomination. Brian has called our attention to quotations that express this truth. In a broad, encompassing sense, God sees a church on earth that we do not see, for He reads every heart. "The Lord knoweth them that are His" (2 Timothy 2:19).

Notice the wording in this passage:

"Notwithstanding the spiritual darkness and alienation from God that exist in the churches which constitute Babylon, the great body of Christ's true followers are still to be found in their communion" (*The Great Controversy*, p. 390).

From God's perspective, the vast majority of His "true followers" are members of the various churches that compose Babylon. This is why the Lord affectionately refers to them as "My people" when He calls them to come out of Babylon (see Revelation 18:4). With our limited human vision we don't know who's who. Only God sees all of His faithful ones the world over. In this sense we could say that the Lord has an *invisible church,* obvious to Him but hidden from our view at present.

But this is not the whole picture regarding God's church in the Spirit of Prophecy. While Ellen White clearly teaches that God has an invisible church, made up of only faithful souls, at the same time she recognized that God also has what she calls "the visible church" (*Testimonies,* vol. 4, p. 16).

Who makes up "the visible church?"

No need to speculate. The very context to this

terminology makes her meaning clear, defining the identity of God's "visible church" on earth:

"The *members* of the church of Christ should be united in one symmetrical body, subject to the sanctified intelligence of the whole.

"The advancement of the church is retarded by *the wrong course of its members. Uniting with the church, although an important and necessary act,* does not make one a Christian nor ensure salvation. We cannot secure a title to heaven by having our names enrolled upon *the church books* while our hearts are alienated from Christ. . . .

"Our profession is an exalted one. As *Sabbathkeeping Adventists* we profess to obey all God's commandments and to be looking for the coming of our Redeemer. . . .

"We should all feel our individual responsibility as *members of the visible church* and workers in the vineyard of the Lord. . . .

"God is leading out a people to stand in perfect unity upon the platform of eternal truth. Christ gave Himself to the world that He might 'purify unto Himself a peculiar people, zealous of good works.' This refining process is designed to *purge the church from all unrighteousness and the spirit of discord and contention,* that they may build up instead of tear down, and concentrate their energies on the great work before them. . . .

"Many do not realize *the sacredness of church relationship* and are loath to submit to *restraint* and *discipline.* Their course of action shows that they exalt their own judgment above that of the united church, and they are not careful to guard themselves lest they encourage a spirit of opposition to *its voice.* Those who hold *responsible positions in the church* may have faults in common with other people and may err in their decisions; but notwithstanding this, the church of Christ on earth has given to them an *authority* that cannot be lightly esteemed. . . .

"*Church relationship is not to be lightly canceled;* yet when the path of some professed followers of Christ is crossed, or when their voice has not the controlling influence which they think it deserves, they will threaten to *leave the church.* . . .

"Every believer should be wholehearted in his attachment to the church. Its prosperity should be his first interest, and unless he feels under sacred obligations to make his connection with the church a benefit to it in preference to himself, it can do far better without him. . . . They are willing to receive all the benefit of its privileges, but prefer to leave others to *pay the bills.* . . . They should defer their *individual judgment* to the *judgment of the body* of the church. . . .

"Let individual *judgment* submit to the *authority* of the church" (*Testimonies,* vol. 4, pp. 16-19; emphasis supplied).

According to this contextual surrounding, the "visible church" is:

- A church in which a person can hold "membership"
- A church whose "members" may pursue a "wrong course"

- A church that maintains a "church book," or membership record
- A church of "Sabbathkeeping Adventists"
- A church that God subjects to a "refining process" to purge out all "unrighteousness, discord and contention"
- A church that has "authority" to impose "restraint and discipline" by the "judgment" of its "voice"
- A church in which its members "hold responsible positions"
- A church you can "leave" by canceling your membership
- A church that must "pay the bills"
- A church whose "authority" is to bear sway over "individual judgment"

Have any guesses as to what Ellen White means when she speaks of God's "visible church"? Beyond any shadow of doubt she means the organized Seventh-day Adventist Church with its worldwide membership and leadership, operating under a heaven ordained system of authority and discipline.

The visible church is visible because it is a recognizable organization with a definable system of order capable of granting or canceling memberships. It elects leadership, carries forth an obvious mission, and bears a name by which it may be identified by the world. The visible church is composed of both wheat and tares, faithful and unfaithful members. A person is not saved by virtue of membership in the visible church, but it is a sacred privilege that should not be taken lightly, for the visible church is the corporate depository of divine truth.

The invisible church, on the other hand, is invisible in the sense that God alone sees each truly faithful soul on earth. This church is not an organized movement. You cannot hold membership in it. There are no earthly books that maintain a record of its names. It has no human leadership, no planned mission, and no system of discipline. The invisible church is composed of only true wheat, with not one tare.

We could illustrate like this:

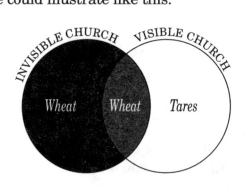

Notice in the above illustration that the invisible church is composed of only wheat, whereas the visible church is composed of both wheat and tares. The two circles overlap because the majority of the wheat are scattered in the various churches and nations of the world, and yet some of the wheat are to be found in the visible church. As we will see in a moment, it is God's ultimate plan to cleanse the visible church of all its unfaithful members and bring all the faithful of the invisible church into the visible church to replace them. The end-product will be a visible church composed of only faithful, true-hearted members.

In order to demonstrate how this transition will occur we need to become familiar with some additional terminology. Carefully notice the wording of the following quotations, giving special attention to "the church militant/church triumphant" concept:

"Has God no living church? He has a church, but it is the church militant not the church triumphant. We are sorry that there are defective members. While the Lord brings into the church those who are truly converted, Satan at the same time brings persons who are not converted into its fellowship. While Christ is sowing the good seed, Satan is sowing the tares. There are two opposing influences continually exerted on the members of the church. One influence is working for the purification of the church, and the other for the corrupting of the people of God" (*The Faith I Live By,* p. 305).

"The church upon the earth is not perfect. The church militant is not the church triumphant. Earth is not heaven. The church is composed of erring men and women who will need patient, painstaking effort, that they may be educated, trained, and disciplined by precept and example, to do their work with acceptance here in this life, and to be crowned with glory and immortality in the future life" (*Manuscript Releases,* vol. 9, p. 154).

In these inspired passages the church is described as having two phases of existence in the world: (1) The Church Militant and (2) The Church Triumphant.

Presently we are in the militant phase of the church's sojourn on earth. It is portrayed as militant because it is engaged in spiritual warfare. Christ brings into the church those who are truly convert-ed, while Satan is on his own evangelistic campaign to bring those who are not converted into its fellow-ship. As a result, there are two opposing influences active in the church. One influence works to cor-rupt, the other to purify. But please note, despite its state of conflict, it is this church—the visible, mili-tant, organized Seventh-day Adventist Church—that is regarded by the Lord as "the light of the world." It is this church—not a church free from evil, but a church in which evils exist— that is "the only object upon the earth upon which Christ bestows His supreme regard." This is not merely my opinion; this is what the Spirit of Prophecy teaches.

There are many today who are surprised by the wrongs that occur in the visible church. They seem to think that there was a former time, in Ellen White's day perhaps, when the church was free from evil influences. They point to the present prob-lems in the church as support for starting or joining separation movements. But the Spirit of Prophecy clearly teaches that the church militant has always been infected with evil influences and will be until it becomes the church triumphant.

In the light of this reality Ellen White warns us not to confuse the militant and triumphant phases of the churches experience:

"Those who think that the church militant is the church triumphant make a great mistake. The church militant will gain great triumphs, but it will also have fierce conflicts with evil that it may be firmly established upon the platform of eternal truth. And every one of us should be determined to stand with the church on this platform" *(Upward Look,* p. 152).

So where and when does *the church triumphant* come into the picture?

Ellen White employs *the church triumphant* terminology to describe the church at that imminent point of its history when it will emerge before the world as both "visible" and "faithful." Prior to this time the visible church has been a mixture of faithful and unfaithful members. The invisible church, though composed of only faithful souls, was hidden to the world's view. But now, for the first time in history, God will have a visibly triumphant church to stand as His faithful witness before the world.

But the visible church will not arise as the triumphant church without a struggle. A painful and almost devastating separation will occur. Carefully notice *how* the separation will occur:

"The church [militant] may appear as about to fall, but it does not fall. It remains [triumphant], while the sinners in Zion will be sifted out—the chaff separated from the precious wheat. This is a terrible ordeal, but nevertheless it must take place. None but those who have been overcoming by the blood of the Lamb and the word of their testimony will be found with the loyal and true, without spot or stain of sin, without guile in their mouths. We must be divested of our self-righteousness and arrayed in the righteousness of Christ" *(Selected Messages,* vol. 2, p. 380; words in brackets supplied).

"As the storm approaches, a large class who have professed faith in the third angel's message, but have not been sanctified through obedience to the truth, abandon their position and join the ranks of the opposition" (*The Great Controversy,* p. 608).

There are those today who are suggesting, even proclaiming with bold authority, that God would have His faithful ones separate themselves from God's visible, organized church. Such a position can only be taken at the denial of inspired counsel. The above quotations and many others clearly tell us *how* the ultimate separation will occur. The unfaithful will abandon their position and join the ranks of the opposition. The unfaithful will take the initiative to separate from the faithful in the visible church. The faithful will not choose to separate from the visible church and leave it to the control of the unfaithful. The ordeal will be so terrible that the church will appear as about to crumble into nonexistence. But it will remain, while the sinners in the visible church will be sifted out, leaving behind what will then constitute the long awaited church triumphant.

The final outcome?

"The members of the church militant who have proved faithful will become the church triumphant" (*Evangelism,* p. 707). Not only will the faithful members of the visible church militant be a part of the church triumphant, but the invisible faithful will unite with them at this time. "Multitudes will receive the faith and join the armies of the Lord" (*Ibid.,* p. 700).

Under the guiding influence of the Holy spirit, every true child of God will eventually be united together as one body of faithful believers. The message of truth for these last days, the third angels message, which lays all human glory in the dust by exalting the Savior as the only hope of salvation, will repel the false-hearted and unite the true followers of Jesus.

The following illustrations depict the entire scenario as inspiration describes it:

### The Present Situation

The majority of God's faithful followers are now invisible to human eyes, while the visible church is composed of both faithful and unfaithful members.

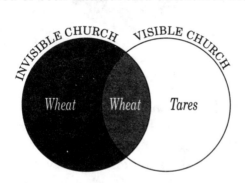

### The Transition

The unfaithful (tares) will abandon their position in the visible church.

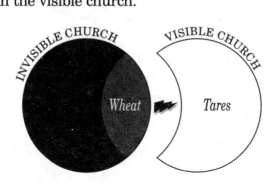

### The Final Outcome

The invisible faithful will join the ranks of the faithful who remain in the visible church, and together they will become the visible church triumphant.

Remember Brian?

With his few quotations, defining the church as faithful souls, he separated from the Seventh-day Adventist Church and has led many others to do the same. After I began to understand the broader context of the church issue, I shared my findings with him. We began with, shall I say, a highly charged exchange of thoughts. Finally, the quotations identifying the organized Seventh-day Adventist denomination as God's visible church prevailed. Brian became calm and emotional. With tears he confessed that his position was not supportable when all Ellen White's comments are considered. I was elated. But then something slipped out of Brian's mouth that startled me to the point of causing my stomach to ache.

"I know what you're saying is true, but I've published so many books declaring the church to be

Babylon. I could never explain to all those people that I was wrong."

Quickly he regained his composure and began defending his position again. I pled with Brian, but to no avail. He was caught in a snare too strong for most men—the pride of opinion. It all began by drawing conclusions with inadequate study. With a few one-side-of-the-issue quotations, Brian declared his position as incontrovertible truth. When added inspired material pointed out the error of his position, he had only one of two options: He could humble himself before the Lord and confess his waywardness, or he could brace himself with pride and evade the clear will of God.

Brian chose the later option, I'm sorry to say.

CHAPTER FOUR
# *Reformation or Anarchy*

Reformation and anarchy can sometimes appear frighteningly similar at first glance. By definition the two words are extremely different. Reform implies a good cause pursued by means of good principles: "to put an end to an evil by enforcing or introducing a better method or course of action" (*Webster's Ninth New Collegiate Dictionary*). Anarchy implies a bad cause pursued by bad principles: "a state of lawlessness or political disorder due to the absence of governmental authority" (*Ibid.*). The difficulty of discerning between the two doesn't arise in the dictionary, but in the claims of anarchy. A movement of anarchy rarely, if ever, openly introduces itself as anarchy. It would gain few followers by an honest disclosure of its true purpose. To be successful anarchy must claim to be reformation!

Most Seventh-day Adventists would agree that the church is in need of revival and reformation.

# Abandon Ship?

The Spirit of Prophecy affirms this perceived need:

"A revival of true godliness among us is the greatest and most urgent of all our needs. To seek this should be our first work. . . .

"A revival and a reformation must take place, under the ministration of the Holy Spirit" (*Selected Messages,* vol. 1, pp. 121, 128).

Yes, Ellen White called for revival and reformation. But are you aware that she also warned of "a condition of anarchy and wild uncertainty" that "will seek to pervade all our ranks of Seventh-day Adventists"? (Letter 40a, 1897). In other words, the Seventh-day Adventist Church is going to experience an uprising of internal forces that will attempt to break down its system of organization and abandon the legitimate, God-ordained authority of its leadership. A spirit of independence will threaten to fragment the church into a disorderly array of autonomous movements. Church members will become wildly uncertain as to the church's standing and authority.

Sound familiar?

On another occasion Ellen White explained that an extreme exercise of independence is the cause of anarchy:

"If the world sees a perfect harmony existing in the church of God, it will be a powerful evidence to them in favor of the Christian religion. Dissensions, unhappy differences, and petty church trials dishonor our Redeemer. All these may be avoided if self is surrendered to God and the followers of Jesus obey the voice of the church. Unbelief suggests that individual independence increases our importance, that it is weak to yield our own ideas of what is right

and proper to the verdict of the church; but to yield
to such feelings and views is unsafe and will bring
us into anarchy and confusion. . . . Let individual
judgment submit to the authority of the church"
(*Testimonies for the Church,* vol. 4, p. 19).

The principles here expressed speak so directly
to some professed reformers that I would venture to
say they will find it hard to believe Ellen White really said such things. "Obey the voice of the church"?
"Individual independence . . . will bring us into
anarchy and confusion"? "Let individual judgment
submit to the authority of the church"? Did she really write such things? Yes, and if you think the ideas
expressed in this quotation are heavy, your head
will really spin when you read this:

"The Redeemer of the world does not sanction
experience and exercise in religious matters independent of His organized and acknowledged
church" (*Sketches for the Life of Paul,* p. 31).

If I were to simply make this kind of statement
as a personal opinion, without any quote marks to
indicate its inspired source, many would ardently
disagree and accuse me of "popery!" But because
these are words Ellen White penned under the
guidance of the Holy Spirit, it necessary for us to
reckon with them. The plain, unavoidable fact is,
God does have a visible, organized church on this
earth, and He has invested that church with a certain degree of authority. Intellectual integrity
demands that anyone who claims to believe in the
Spirit of Prophecy acknowledge this reality. To pursue religious matters independent of God's organized church is not sanctioned by Christ and opens

the way for anarchy. We are not dealing here with a light matter. Ponder the words again: "The Redeemer of the world does not sanction experience and exercise in religious matters independent of His organized and acknowledged church."

The danger warned against in this statement is independence, which automatically brings to mind independent ministries. Now before you conclude that you know what I'm going to say, please hear me out. Do not assume that I'm attempting to out-rightly condemn independent ministries. That would be hard for me to do since I am myself an associate/director of an independent ministry.

I have had to grapple with the issue of independence with regards to God's "organized and acknowledged church." There was a time when the independence of the independent ministry I work for was tending toward anarchy. We did not understand the principles laid down in the above quotations. We thought our independence was a virtue. In reality, it was a weakness. Once we finally realized our danger, we decided to change our attitude and obey the inspired counsel regarding our relationship to God's church.

It was shortly after we made this decision that I began to see the fine line between reformation and anarchy. The true reformation God desires for the Seventh-day Adventist Church will not break the church up into independent atoms or forsake the church to form a new movement. Ellen White makes this clear beyond controversy:

"I know that the Lord loves His church. It is not to be disorganized or broken up into independent atoms. There is not the least consistency in this; there is not the least evidence that such a thing will be" (*The Remnant Church,* p. 53).

"We cannot now step off the foundation that God has established. We cannot now enter into any new organization; for this would mean apostasy from the truth" (*Selected Messages,* vol. 2, p. 390).

"God has a church upon the earth, who are His chosen people, who keep His commandments. He is leading, not stray off-shoots, not one here and one there, but a people" (*Review and Herald,* vol. 3, p. 82).

In response to inspired counsel like this some independent individuals have suggested that Ellen White's positive statements about the organized church no longer apply due to the present condition of the church. She wrote nothing, they suggest, that indicates the Seventh-day Adventist Church would continue on as God's recognized movement until the end of time. But the fact is, she did receive prophetic counsel from the Lord regarding the future of this church:

"I am instructed to say to Seventh-day Adventists the world over, God has called us as a people to be a peculiar treasure unto Himself. He has appointed that His church on earth shall stand perfectly united in the Spirit and counsel of the Lord of hosts *to the end of time*" (*Selected Messages,* vol. 2, p. 397; italics supplied).

"No advice or sanction is given in the Word of God to those who believe the third angel's message to lead them to suppose that they can draw apart. This you may settle with yourselves forever. It is the devising of unsanctified minds that would encourage a state of disunion. . . .

"There must be no separating [of the faithful from the church] in this great testing time" (*Selected Messages,* vol. 3, p. 21; words in brackets added for contextual clarity).

Words couldn't be much plainer. It is God's plan that the same organized church of which Ellen White was a member in her day shall continue as His peculiar treasure "to the end of time." We are not to "draw apart." There will be no divinely led "separating." Just to make sure we wouldn't misunderstand how long this counsel will apply, she adds for good measure, "This you may settle with yourselves *forever.*"

I know there is someone reading this who is worried that such quotations seem to overlook the conditional nature of God's promises. After all, Israel was God's chosen nation. He promised her that she would stand forever as His people, but they closed their probation and forfeited the promise. He then called out His faithful ones to form the Christian church. With time, the church became corrupt and God raised up reformers to separate and form Protestantism. Then Protestantism failed and God raised up the Adventist church to call out His true people. Certainly we should not be surprised if Adventism fails and the faithful have to separate again. The pattern is consistent throughout history. Why not now?

But listen. It is precisely here that the end-time scenario is, indeed, different.

The cycle of

- God choosing a people to be His church,
- that church failing in its mission,
- and God calling out the faithful to start a new movement,

obviously must be broken before the great controversy between good and evil can end. Ultimately, God must have a people who will triumph with the gospel and not fail. And He will have such a people. The divine agenda reveals that this vital transition from failure to triumph will occur with the Advent movement.

Think it through with me.

While God did call Israel to be His people and did make promises to her, He also made it clear that her days were numbered to fulfill certain conditions. Daniel 9:24 clearly allotted a period of seventy weeks as a probationary limit for Israel. According to Daniel's prophecy the coming of the Messiah would constitute the final test for the Jewish nation. When they rejected Christ and persecuted His followers, their probation closed and the New Testament church was born. Israel's failure did not catch God by surprise. Prophecy made provision for that tragedy. But no such provision exists in the end-time prophetic scenario concerning the Advent movement. There is no inspired word, either in the Bible or the Spirit of Prophecy, that foretells the failure of the Advent movement and the rising of another. According to Revelation, which is the last book of the Bible, the prophetic agenda reads like this:

- The apostolic church replaces Israel (see Revelation 12:1, 2).
- The Christian church is displaced by a massive counterfeit system, by which the faithful are persecuted (see Revelation 12:6, 12-15).
- The remnant church emerges in America and the dragon makes war on her (see Revelation 12:16, 17).
- The remnant church passes through a great disappointment but rises out of it to prophecy again before many nations and languages (see Revelation 10).
- The great, final test comes upon the world as the remnant church proclaims the three angel's messages (see Revelation 13 and 14).
- The harvest of the earth is reaped and Jesus returns (see Revelation 14:14-20).

That's the whole story as it appears in prophecy. There is absolutely no indication that this scenario is conditional or that another movement beyond the remnant will arise.

The very same conclusion is clear in the earlier prophecy of the seven churches. Each successive church reveals the progressive developments and transitions that God's people experience down through history. Ephesus introduces the early apostolic church. Pergamos and Thyatira reveal the formation and fall of the papacy. Sardis brings to view the rise and fall of Protestantism. Philadelphia presents the birth of Adventism and the opening of the judgment in heaven. Finally, Laodicea concludes the picture by describing the lukewarm condition that would paralyze Adventism. A divine diagnosis is made. A remedy is prescribed. And a promise of high honor is given to all who overcome the sleepy plight of Laodicea. But no denunciation is issued.

There are only seven churches, not eight. Seven is the prophetic number for completion, which indicates that God will finish His plan within the framework of the seven churches with no need for an eighth. The cycle of rising and falling churches ends with the seventh church. Some overcome and some do not, but no new movement emerges.

Both the remnant church in Revelation 12 and the Laodicean church in Revelation 3 are identified by the Spirit of Prophecy as symbolic representations of the organized Seventh-day Adventist Church. This being the case, logic drives us to the conclusion that the Seventh-day Adventist Church will continue as God's recognized movement until "the end of time." To draw any other conclusion would be to believe that God's prophetic glance failed to see all the way down to our time and beyond. It would also require us to venture out beyond what is written in prophecy and take a blind leap into a new movement nowhere foretold in the word of God. The One who knows the end from the beginning just doesn't work that way. "Surely the Lord God will do nothing, but He revealeth His secret unto His servants the prophets" (Amos 3:7).

I can hear someone asking, "But what about all the problems in the church—the compromises, the scandals, the theological conflicts, the worldliness? How will the Lord deal with all this if He won't start all over with a new movement?"

# Abandon Ship?

It is vital that we understand the inspired answer to this question. The Lord clearly tells us exactly how He will handle the situation. There is a separation on God's agenda. Be certain of that. But it will be different than all previous separations. In the past God has dealt with the mixture of faithful and unfaithful members in His church by a "calling out." The faithful were called to take the initiative to separate from the unfaithful and start a new church. But if this cycle were to continue indefinitely, good would never triumph over evil. In the final scenario something entirely new occurs. Rather than another "calling out" of the faithful, this time the church will undergo a "shaking out" of the unfaithful. There is a major difference between these two methods of separation. Notice:

"There will be a shaking of the sieve. *The chaff must in time be separated from the wheat.* Because iniquity abounds, the love of many waxes cold. It is the very time when the genuine will be strongest. There will be *a separating from us* of those who have not appreciated the light nor walked in it" (Letter 46, 1887, p. 6; emphasis supplied).

What will the shaking of the church accomplish? "The chaff" (the unfaithful who are presently in the church) will be "separated" from "the wheat" (the faithful in the church). The unfaithful will separate from the church, not the faithful!

"As the storm approaches, a large class who have professed faith in the third angel's message, but have not been sanctified through obedience to the truth, *abandon their position* and join the ranks of the opposition" (*The Great Controversy,* p. 608; emphasis supplied).

Who will abandon their position and join other ranks? The unfaithful.

"Soon God's people will be tested by fiery trials, and the great proportion of those who now appear to be genuine and true will prove to be base metal. Instead of being strengthened and confirmed by opposition, threats, and abuse, *they will cowardly take the side of the opposers. . . .*

"To stand in defense of truth and righteousness when *the majority forsake us,* to fight the battles of the Lord when champions are few—this will be our test. At this time we must gather warmth from the coldness of others, courage from their cowardice, and loyalty from their treason" (*Testimonies for the Church,* vol. 5, p. 136; emphasis supplied).

Who will forsake who? The unfaithful will forsake the faithful!

"The church may appear as about to fall, but it does not fall. It remains, while *the sinners in Zion will be sifted out—the chaff separated from the precious wheat.* This is a terrible ordeal, but nevertheless it must take place" (*Selected Messages,* vol. 2, p. 380; emphasis supplied).

Will the church fall? No! Who will be sifted out? The chaff!

Those who advocate separation from the church, either openly or subtlety, are working in direct conflict with God's final plan to conquer evil. They think they are defending truth and claim to be bringing about reformation, but they are missing one vital element of the divine game-plan. In the final episode of the great controversy, the church will constitute a framework in which every member will undergo a development of character in preparation for the great, final test that will prove each one faithful or unfaithful. The church is God's theater of grace in which the final issues of the great controversy will be acted out.

Give careful consideration to this inspired insight:

"Although in our churches, that claim to believe advanced truth, there are those who are faulty and erring, as tares among the wheat, God is long-suffering and patient. He reproves and warns the erring, but He does not destroy those who are long in learning the lesson He would teach them; He does not uproot the tares from the wheat. Tares and wheat are to grow together till the harvest; when the wheat comes to its full growth and development, and because of its character when ripened, it will be fully distinguished from the tares" (*Testimonies to Ministers,* pp. 45, 46).

The principle upon which God is working is to allow the unfaithful and the faithful to develop character in close proximity to one another, in church relation. Both are engaged in a ripening process to be culminated when the character of God's faithful ones is fully distinguished from the unfaithful. The differences, the conflicts, the theological wars, virtually every relationship, every trial and every temptation brought to bear upon the church provide an opportunity for character formation.

- Some are gradually adapting to the world, compromising principle and cultivating unbelief in God's word.
- Others are responding to the evil influences that creep into the church by cultivating a spirit of condemnation and self-righteousness while secretly cherishing their own pet sins and failing to walk in genuine consecration to the Lord.
- Somewhere in the midst of all the compromise and conflict, there are those who refuse to entertain evil and yet refrain from accusing and condemning others. They uphold truth and righteousness in the spirit of Christ.

Finally, the great, climactic test will come. Every foundation will be shaken to reveal cherished virtue or hidden evil. God has ordained *a specific time* and has designed *a specific test* that will accurately separate the wheat and the tares into two distinct groups. Don't miss this inspired insight:

"*The time* is not far distant when *the test* will come to every soul. The mark of the beast will be urged upon us. Those who have step by step yielded to worldly demands and conformed to worldly customs will not find it a hard matter to yield to the powers that be, rather than subject themselves to derision, insult, threatened imprisonment, and death. The contest is between the commandments of God and the commandments of men. *In this time* the gold will be separated from the dross in the church" (*Testimonies for the Church,* vol. 5, p. 81; italics supplied).

According to this quotation, the separation of the gold and the dross in the church is scheduled for the time when the mark of the beast is urged upon us. Until then, the members of the church, whether knowing or unknowing, are preparing for victory or defeat as that final test approaches. All are now maturing as either wheat or tares. Any effort to bring about a separation prior to *that time* and *that test* which God has built into His plan will prove incapable of discerning between those who are truly faithful and those who are not. Premature separatist movements run the risk of uprooting precious wheat as they go about trying to uproot tares. And once any movement separates from the church, it will soon be discovered that some of the wheat and tares have simply gathered together in a new group. The desired objective of establishing an all-faithful new church will fail, because God is not in it. He has *His time* and *His test* planned. Every other separation is the work of the enemy of souls.

There are two kinds of separatist movements confronting the church at the present time. One is very open and clear as to its intent. Their message is unmistakable:

"The organized Seventh-day Adventist Church is now a part of Babylon and all who are faithful must separate from her or be lost."

Those who take this position assemble quotations from the Spirit of Prophecy for their support. But somehow they have overlooked one simple fact: Ellen White died a member of the Seventh-day Adventist Church! This one historical reality forces us to an all too obvious conclusion: If the life-long

example of Ellen White reveals faithful membership in the church, and it does, then there is nothing she ever wrote that was meant to be taken as a
call to separate from the church. To compile sen-
tences and paragraphs from her writings to make it
appear as though she was in favor of separation
lacks either intelligence or integrity, for such an
interpretation of her words attempts to make her
say something that her church membership contra-
dicts. To use her writings to support separation
from the Seventh-day Adventist Church would be
like using the writings of Moses to prove Israel was
not God's chosen nation. The fact that he continued
leading them through the wilderness would ever
contradict the vain attempt.

While Ellen White was still living, there was a
man by the name of Stanton who was denouncing
the organized church as Babylon and calling the
faithful to separate. To accomplish his mission he
was quoting heavily from the Spirit of Prophecy.
Ellen wrote him a letter of straight rebuke. Notice
these excerpts:

"Dear Brother Stanton: I address to you a few
lines. I am not in harmony with the position that
you have taken; for I have been shown by the Lord
that just such position will be taken by those who
are in error. . . .

"My brother, I learn that you are taking the
position that the Seventh-day Adventist Church is
Babylon, and that all that would be saved must
come out of her. You are not the only man whom the
enemy has deceived in this matter. For the last forty
years, one man after another has arisen, claiming

that the Lord has sent him with the same message; but let me tell you, as I have told them, that this message you are proclaiming is one of the Satanic delusions designed to create confusion among the churches. My brother, you are certainly off the track. . . .

"My brother, if you are teaching that the Seventh-day Adventist Church is Babylon, you are wrong. God has not given you any such message to bear. Satan will use every mind to which he can attain access, inspiring men to originate false theories, or go off on some wrong tangent, that he may create a false excitement, and thus diverts souls from the true issue for this time. I presume that some may be deceived by your message, because they are full of curiosity and desire for some new thing. . . .

"Do not seek to misinterpret, and twist, and pervert, the testimonies to substantiate any such message of error. Many have passed over this ground, and have done great harm. As others have started up full of zeal to proclaim this message, again and again, I have been shown that it was not truth" (*Review and Herald,* vol. 3, p. 82).

We can only conclude that those who use the Spirit of Prophecy to support a position of separation are either very sloppy students or they are compromising their moral integrity by falsely representing Ellen White's intent.

But I said there are two kinds of separatist movements. The second one I have in mind is not so blatant as the first. In fact, we could refer to this group as *the separatists who don't believe in separation.* The prominent voices in this movement claim they believe the Seventh-day Adventist Church is still God's one and only true church, but for all practical purposes they are separated from the church. They confess the obvious truth of inspiration:

"The Seventh-day Adventist Church is God's true church. The church is not Babylon. We must not separate."

But the practical, tangible proof of that professed conviction is mysteriously missing. Reality looks more like this:

"This is God's church, but we need to start home churches."

"This is God's church, but we can't support it."

"This is God's church, but its leaders have no authority."

"This is God's church, but we cannot work in cooperative relationship with it."

"This is God's church, but the burden of our message is to proclaim its failures."

I think you see what I mean.

When asked to define their mission, they will claim to be those through whom God is working to bring about reformation in the church. But the course they pursue for *reformation* looks more like the independence that leads to *anarchy* warned against in the Spirit of Prophecy. Why do they not feel a burden to reckon with inspired counsel like this:

"While it is true that the Lord guides individuals, it is also true that He is leading out a people, not a few separate individuals here and there, one believing this thing, another that. Angels of God are doing the work committed to their trust. The third angel is leading out and purifying a people, and they should move with him unitedly. . . .

"The spirit of pulling away from our fellow laborers, the spirit of disorganization, is in the very air we breathe. By some, all efforts to establish order are regarded as dangerous—as a restriction of personal liberty, and hence to be feared as popery. They declare that they will not take any man's say-so; that they are amenable to no man. I have been instructed that it is Satan's special effort to lead men to feel that God is pleased to have them choose their own course, independent of the counsel of their brethren. . . .

"Oh, how Satan would rejoice if he could succeed in his efforts to get in among this people and disorganize the work at a time when thorough organization is essential and will be the greatest power to keep out spurious uprisings and to refute claims not endorsed by the word of God! We want to hold the lines evenly, that there shall be no breaking down of the system of organization and order that has been built up by wise, careful labor. License must not be given to disorderly elements that desire to control the work at this time.

"Some have advanced the thought that as we near the close of time, every child of God will act independently of any religious organization. But I have been instructed by the Lord that in this work there is no such thing as every man's being independent. . . .

"In order that the Lord's work may advance healthfully and solidly, His people must draw together. . . .

"If men will not move in concert in the great and grand work for this time, there will be confusion. It is not a good sign when men refuse to unite with their brethren and prefer to act alone. Instead of isolating themselves, let them draw in harmony with their fellow laborers. Unless they do this, their activity will work at the wrong time and in the wrong way. They will often work counter to that which God would have done, and thus their labor is worse than wasted" (*Testimonies to Ministers,* pp. 488-490).

The answer given to this counsel has been, "We have tried to work with the church, but the apostasy is so great that it is impossible to preach the truth within the structure. They don't want to hear it."

At one time this alibi sounded pretty righteous and sincere to me. But then the Lord showed me that it was at best a mere fear of an unreality, and at worse a shady excuse for disobedience to the inspired counsel.

May I offer a personal testimony regarding the matter?

In 1992 the board of Light Bearers Ministry, which is the *supportive* independent ministry I represent as associate director/speaker, voted unanimously to decline all tithe support from Seventh-day Adventist members and to work in cooperative relationship with the church. After much study and prayer we felt strongly convicted that God would have us do all we could, short of compromising principle, to conduct our ministry in harmony with the mission and counsel of the church. Our heartfelt purpose has been to obey the inspired word concerning this issue and to occupy a humble position of submission to the church body.

Other independent ministries responded to our decision with shock and opposition. They warned us that church leaders would try to control our ministry, our preaching, even our theological convictions. We are *almost* certain that such diabolical papists do exist in the church, although we have not yet encountered any. All we have received from church leaders is respect, encouragement and urgent requests to keep right on publishing and preaching.

Of course we are very happy that the prophecies of doom have not come true. However, we made our decision because we believed it was the right thing to do, not to receive encouragement from church leaders. God has blessed abundantly. We now have the wonderful privilege of working for revival and reformation *in* the church, along with all the many other leaders and members who share that aspiration. They do exist.

Reformation is a real need.

Anarchy is a real danger.

I invite you to pray and labor for the one and urge you to beware of the other.

CHAPTER FIVE

# A Corporate Affair

All Seventh-day Adventists, especially those of the more conservative persuasion, believe that we are living in the antitypical day of atonement. Some who lean extra far right have pointed to this great truth as justification for taking a position of separation from the church.

The reasoning goes something like this:

"We are now living in the solemn, antitypical day of atonement. On that day in the ancient type, Israel was to put away all sin from the camp in order to receive the final atonement. The organized church is failing to engage in this cleansing work. There is sin in the camp, so we must separate from the camp and seek the Lord individually."

There is at least one major problem with this line of reasoning: the day of atonement was not primarily an individual matter. It was a corporate affair.

Allow me to explain.

# Abandon Ship?

The sanctuary service was divided into two phases of ministration: (1) The daily service and (2) the yearly service.

The daily service was, indeed, an individual matter. Day by day throughout the year the Israelite people brought their individual sacrifices to the sanctuary to seek atonement for their individual sins. Each sinner manifested personal repentance and made personal confession for his or her personal violations of God's law. The service had little or nothing to do with the Jewish church as a body. The primary concern was ones personal standing with the Lord.

The day of atonement was different in its focus. On that solemn day each year the entire congregation was to present itself before the Lord as a single man, as one body. Rather than each individual bringing a sacrifice for his personal sins, one sacrifice was made for all the people as though they all shared the same guilt; and, in fact, they did, which was the point. No one stood apart to claim any higher standing than the body as a whole. No one sought to approach God on his own to receive what the day of atonement offered. In fact, anyone who refused to answer the call for a united approach to Jehovah was cut off from the camp as a lost soul. Oh yes, there was a personal preparation necessary for the day, but the point is that when the day finally arrived it was a corporate affair.

The prophet Joel helps us understand the corporate focus of the day of atonement:

"Blow the trumpet in Zion, sanctify a fast, call a solemn assembly: gather the people, sanctify the congregation, assemble the elders, gather the children, and those that suck the breasts: let the bridegroom go forth of his chamber, and the bride out of her closet. Let the priests, the ministers of the Lord, weep between the porch and the altar, and let them say, Spare Thy people, O Lord, and give not thine heritage to reproach, that the heathen should rule over them: wherefore should they say among the people, Where is their God? Then will the Lord be jealous for His land, and pity His people. Yea, the Lord will answer and say unto His people, Behold, I will send you corn, and wine, and oil, and ye shall be satisfied therewith: and I will no more make you a reproach among the heathen: . . .

"Fear not, O land; be glad and rejoice: for the Lord will do great things. Be not afraid, ye beasts of the field: for the pastures of the wilderness do spring, for the tree beareth her fruit, the fig tree and the vine do yield their strength. Be glad then, ye children of Zion, and rejoice in the Lord your God: for He hath given you the former rain moderately, and He will cause to come down for you the rain, the former rain, and the latter rain in the first month. And ye shall eat in plenty, and be satisfied, and praise the name of the Lord your God, that hath dealt wondrously with you: and My people shall never be ashamed. And ye shall know that I am in the midst of Israel, and that I am the Lord your God, and none else: and My people shall never be ashamed" (Joel 2:15-19, 21-23, 26, 27).

A careful consideration of this prophecy sheds much valuable light on God's purpose in this great day of atonement. It reveals, as well, how He would

81

have us conduct ourselves in view of that purpose. There are three key points I'd like to highlight:

**1. A call to unify, not to separate:**

According to Joel's prophecy, the trumpet of truth will be blown "in Zion," not by self-appointed messengers who stand on the outside shouting in. The message of the Lord is to be heard *in* the church, proclaimed by those who are clearly identifiable as part of the corporate body. Joel is clear, as well, that we will know the sound of the true trumpet because it will call the church to "assemble," to unify as a people before the Lord, not to fragment into independent atoms.

The purpose for the gathering process is to *"sanctify the congregation."* It is not merely a personal sanctifying we are to seek, as important as that is, but a sanctifying of the church as a body. In order to accomplish His greater purpose in the controversy between good and evil, the Lord must have more than a sanctified *person* here and there. He calls for a sanctified *people,* a body of individuals who are knit together as one to demonstrate the transforming power of divine grace.

**2. A Spirit of Intercession, Not of Condemnation:**

Verse 17 teaches us the attitude we are to possess in this great day of atonement. Joel's prophecy recognizes that the church is not standing in right relation to God. And yet it encourages us to enter into a spirit of intercession on behalf of the church. Intercessory prayer is the divinely appointed means of correcting the situation. Joel calls for a spirit that weeps and pleads for the Lord's acceptance of His failing people rather than a spirit that gives her up to doom.

Those who engage in the spirit of intercession described by Joel do so because they recognize that the honor of God is at stake. Their primary concern is that unbelievers would not find cause to mock, saying, "Where is their God?" For if the church were to fail, the reputation of the Lord we claim to represent would come into disrepute before the world. His truth, His law, His offer of salvation would be cast aside along with the church itself.

### 3. A Future of Triumph, Not of Defeat:

Joel's prophecy is full of hope. According to his inspired insight, "the Lord will pity His people" in response to a spirit of intercession on her behalf. Not only will He pity, but He will abundantly bless the church with "corn and oil and wine," which are symbols of spiritual enrichment. "The Lord will do great things" for His beloved people. He will cause the church to "bear her fruit . . . and yield her strength." She will be revived and receive the long awaited outpouring of the Holy Spirit in "latter rain" power. The Lord will deal "wondrously" with His people, promises Joel, and they will "praise the name of the Lord." The church will arise and shine with the radiance of the Lord's presence and shall "never be ashamed" again.

It is true, and must not be forgotten, that we are saved as individual believers in Christ, not as a denomination. "No denominational name has any virtue to bring us into favor with God. We are saved individually as believers in the Lord Jesus Christ" (*Review and Herald,* February 10, 1891). But as

# Abandon Ship?

Seventh-day Adventists living in the day of atonement, there is something that ought to loom in our hearts as of far greater importance than our personal ticket to heaven. The issue of higher significance is the honor of God's name, the vindication of His character. And a united people, bound together with the Savior's love, is the most persuasive testimony on behalf of God's character that can be given to the world.

The prayer of Christ in John 17 emphasizes just how crucial the unity of the church is to God's ultimate plan for the world. This prayer is of extra special significance for the day of atonement church, for it is the very prayer Christ offers now before the Father as our heavenly High Priest. "This prayer is a lesson regarding the intercession that the Savior would carry on within the veil, when His great sacrifice in behalf of men, the offering of Himself, should have been completed" (*SDA Bible Commentary,* vol. 5, p. 1145). Jesus prayed this prayer of John 17 before His ascension to heaven so we would know the real substance of His intercession on our behalf.

The first issue we encounter in Christ's prayer is *the glory of God.* "I have glorified Thee on the earth: I have finished the work which Thou gavest Me to do. . . . I have manifested Thy name," proclaims the Savior to His Father. The great purpose for which Jesus came into the world was to make known the true character of God and vindicate the honor of His name. He achieved that vital goal by living a sinless life of selfless love and by voluntarily suffering the penalty of our rebellion. His life and death have demonstrated beyond question that God is, indeed, the good and loving Lord He claims Himself to be.

But please notice, Christ does not conclude His prayer by presenting to the Father the immediate accomplishments of His life and death. His prayer extends to encompass the extensive glory that is to flow forth from all He has done.

"I pray for them. . . . and I am glorified in them," says Christ of His church. As Jesus was the medium of glory for the Father, so the church is the medium of glory for the Son. "And now I am no more in the world," He continues, "but these are in the world, and I come to Thee. Holy Father, keep through Thine own name those whom Thou hast given Me, that they may be one, as We are." The Savior's prayer opens to our understanding the practical means through which His glory will illuminate the world. Realizing that He will soon ascend to heaven, Jesus pleads with the Father to preserve the faithfulness of His people "through Thine own name"—that is, through the knowledge of God's true character revealed in Christ. Then He comes to the absolutely crucial matter of unity. The unity of the church is the essential, tangible blessing that comes from knowing God: "That they all may be one; as We are." According to Jesus, it is the oneness of His people that will effectively testify to the glory of His name.

As He continues praying, the theme develops more fully: "That they all may be one; as Thou, Father, art in Me, and I in Thee, that they also may be one in Us: that the world may believe that Thou hast sent Me." The words, "that the world may believe," are a key part of Christ's prayer. He is saying, in essence, that the unity of the church is the powerful influence that will persuade unbelievers to trust Him as their Savior. But why, in practical terms, is the unity of the church such a powerful witness to the world? The climactic words of the Savior's prayer tells us why.

"The world hast not known Thee," Jesus reasons, "but I have known Thee, and these have known that Thou hast sent Me. And I have declared unto them Thy name, and will declare it: that the love wherewith Thou hast loved Me may be in them, and I in them." The thing that deeply troubles Christ is that the world has not known the true character of God. It is this ignorance that holds the world in bondage to Satan, to sin, to selfishness. It is by feeding into the human mind misrepresentations of the divine character that the devil is able to maintain control over his victims.

"But . . ."

Jesus is about to make a vitally contrasting declaration.

"But I have known Thee." The world has not known the Father, but Jesus has. From eternity past He has lived in intimate companionship with the One who dwells in unapproachable light. If anyone knows the true character of God, Jesus does. And so—blessed reality—He came to our darkened world on an urgent mission to reveal the Father's heart. Jesus is totally confident that if fallen men and women can but be led to see God, in all His matchless beauty, they will eagerly yield their loyalty to His maligned kingdom. But how will the world be thus enlightened? The answer to this question is exciting: "That the love wherewith Thou hast loved Me may be in them, and I in them." Do you see, dear friend of Jesus? Through the practical demonstration of God's love in the church Jesus will be exalted before the world.

It's not the perfect sermon that the world needs.

It's not the most spectacular evangelistic program that will make the big difference.

It's not the most attractive publication, mass-produced and circulated around the globe, that will persuade the world that Christ should reign supreme in their hearts.

Oh friend, listen: It's God's love that the world longs to see.

God's love, in you and me, in the church.

God's love, revealing its power to unify fallen, sinful, selfish men and women who have been transformed into the image of Christ.

I can hear someone whispering a passionate Amen. If it's you, then I want to welcome you to the growing number of Seventh-day Adventists who are rejoicing to realize the omnipotent power of divine love. The great system of truth God has given this church is a saving influence only in the illuminating context of that love—that matchless love—as it was declared, displayed and defined in the living and dying of Christ Jesus.

With the prayer of Christ in mind, let's come full circle now, back to the topic of our original interest in this chapter—the corporate nature of the day of atonement.

The reason why the day of atonement is a corporate affair, rather than merely an individual one, is because atonement is a word that means *to be one*. It is a truth that ultimately aims to reconcile fallen man to a holy God, and to reconcile fallen man with fallen man in the church as the practical proof that the atonement is worthy of the world's notice.

The spirit of the atonement is one of united repentance, each member sensing his personal guilt as equal to that of the entire church body. No spirit of "save me and damn them." No attitude of "I'm right and they're wrong." Each member realizes that he or she is as much in need of God's mercy as every other.

The spirit of the atonement is one of united standing before the Lord, each member interceding on behalf of the body as for his or her own soul. The strong hold up the weak. The wise bear patiently with the foolish.

The spirit of the atonement is one that transcends concern for personal salvation and refocuses on the honor of God and the salvation of other souls.

In the largest scope of its influence, the atonement of Christ will ultimately "gather [unite] together in one all things in Christ, both which are in heaven, and which are on earth; even in Him" (Ephesians 1:10; words in brackets supplied). "To the intent that now unto the principalities and powers in heavenly places might be known by the church the manifold wisdom of God" (Ephesians 3:10).

Not only will the unity of the church persuade many in this fallen world to yield their loyalty to Christ, but the convincing testimony of the Savior's love in His people will resound throughout the entire universe. The thinking, reasoning, watching inhabitants of the heavens will behold in Christ, and in His church, the manifold wisdom of God. The universe will be made eternally secure against a second rebellion though the atonement of Christ.

All hearts in heaven and earth will beat in glorious unison. All will proclaim with joyous delight,

> *One God*—the good and loving Father of all creation forever vindicated.
>
> *One kingdom*—the church of Christ on earth and the unfallen intelligences of heaven as one harmonious family.
>
> *One desire*—to adore and worship the One who has proved Himself worthy of our highest loyalty and deepest love.

Will your voice be heard in that vast throng?

# CHAPTER SIX
# *The Great Advent Pendulum*

No doubt you've heard of "the up's and down's." It's a catchy phrase we use to describe an extended period of emotional high's and low's.

And certainly you've heard of "the in's and out's." It's a term used in business and law to simplify what might otherwise be referred to as "the numerous and interrelated rules and exceptions to those rules that govern the legal relationships between individual people and corporate entities." Whew! It's a good thing some jargon exhausted person came up with "the in's and out's" to describe all that.

But have you ever heard of "the back and forth's"? Neither had I, until I needed to come up with a term to describe the spiritual journey of the Seventh-day Adventist Church. It's a term that conjures up pendulum images in my mind. The pendulum of a clock swings back and forth, from right to left. Seems to me, if you don't mind me saying so, that Adventist history has been kind of like that. It's not a distinctly Adventist problem, however. Actually, it's a human problem in general. Notice this insight:

"There is in human nature a tendency to run to extremes and from one extreme to another entirely opposite" (Testimonies for the Church, vol. 5, p. 305).

We should not be surprised, then, that God has commanded us, "Ye shall not turn aside to the right hand or to the left" (Deuteronomy 5:32). The Lord knew we were prone to veer off track into conservative and liberal extremes.

"There are two errors against which the children of God—particularly those who have just come to trust in His grace—especially need to guard. The first . . . is that of looking to their own works, trusting to anything they can do, to bring themselves into harmony with God. . . .

"The opposite and no less dangerous error is that belief in Christ releases men from keeping the law of God; that since by faith alone we become partakers of the grace of Christ, our works have nothing to do with our redemption" (*Steps to Christ,* pp. 59, 60).

The pendulum effect can be seen throughout the entire history of Christianity. Every denomination has struggled to find balance in its theology and spiritual experience. It is my conviction that the balance which has eluded Christianity for centuries will eventually be attained within the framework of

# The Great Advent Pendulum

Adventist theology and experience. The long history of that honorable quest for spiritual equipoise has ever merged toward Adventism, gathering along the way all the necessary elements for the realization of a marvelous reality. It is as if all the vital truths of the ages have pooled together in this one time of history, in this one movement of destiny, to bring forth the crowning manifestation of saving grace, the most persuasive representation of Christ's character the world has ever witnessed. The system of truth embodied in Adventism, when viewed in the light of the cross, has the potential to reveal divine love with unprecedented clarity and beauty. All the ingredients are present. We await synthesis. We anticipate the vital fusion of our distinctive message with the gospel of Christ. We look forward to the rising of the glorious light inherent in Adventism.

Trace the Advent journey with me and I think you'll see both the pendulum and the potential.

The Advent movement was born into a religious climate that was tending to the far left. Protestantism had come out of the hard, cold, legalistic clutches of Catholicism. The rediscovery of justification by faith alone began moving the people in a leftward direction away from the graceless prison of Romanism. It was a necessary shift of focus, but rather than moving only far enough left to find center, the Protestant churches continued moving until they were lethally left of center. Rather than giving works their proper place as the inevitable fruit of faith, they threw out the law altogether. The theory became popular that the grace of Christ has abolished the law, making the ten commandments of no real theological significance after Calvary.

It was here, at this point in Christian history, that Adventism stepped on stage. The new movement made its debut with what we might call a Christ-centered-law-revering faith. That early, pre-disappointment, Millerite movement is described in the Spirit of Prophecy as a revival of apostolic faith.

But as Adventism continued to take shape, the discovery of certain distinctive Bible truths placed the young church in a position where self-defense seemed necessary. The Sabbath, the state of the dead, the sanctuary and the judgment—these and other truths set Adventism apart from mainstream Protestantism. The church came under attack and felt the need to give formidable proof for its theological positions. Because our positions were so supportable from Scripture, it became quite popular and even pleasurable to do battle with the less Biblically astute Protestants. Adventist preaching evolved into a highly skilled proof-text art form devoted to doctrinal debate. Naturally, the primary item of our defense was the law, and the Sabbath in particular, which began to breed into Adventism a heavy obedience-to-the-law emphasis. The church became known for its defense of the law.

Defense of the law was needed, to some degree, but not to the neglect of the gospel of God's free grace in Christ. Unfortunately, that's exactly what happened. Assessing the situation, Ellen White warned that "Many [Seventh-day Adventists] had lost sight of Jesus" (*Testimonies to Ministers,* p. 92; words in brackets supplied). In its zeal to prove to the world that obedience to God's law is necessary, the church made Christ little more than a footnote under what was considered the more important "present truth" message. Book after book was published; sermon after sermon was preached; but Jesus was scarcely mentioned, the gospel hardly commented upon. Ellen White was prompted by the Lord to confront the church with a startling reality:

"On the one hand, religionists generally have divorced the law from the gospel, while we [Adventists] have, on the other hand, almost done the same thing from another standpoint. We have not held up before the people the righteousness of Christ and the full significance of His great plan of redemption. We [Adventists] have left out Christ and His matchless love, brought in theories and reasonings, and preached argumentative discourses. . . .

"The danger has been presented to me again and again of entertaining, as a people, false ideas of justification by faith. I have been shown for years that Satan would work in a special manner to confuse the mind on this point. The law of God has been largely dwelt upon and has been presented to congregations, almost as destitute of the knowledge of Jesus Christ and His relation to the law as was the offering of Cain. I have been shown that many have been kept from the faith because of the mixed, confused ideas of salvation, because the ministers have worked in a wrong manner to reach hearts. The point that has been urged upon my mind for years is the imputed righteousness of Christ. . . .

"There is not a point that needs to be dwelt upon more earnestly, repeated more frequently, or established more firmly in the minds of all than the impossibility of fallen man meriting anything by his own best good works. Salvation is through faith in Jesus Christ alone" (*Faith and Works,* pp. 15, 16, 18, 19; words in brackets supplied).

Obviously there needed to be a change of focus if Adventism was to preach God's final message to the world. To merely prove our distinctive doctrines would never constitute fulfilling the gospel commission. Yes, the distinctive doctrines of the church are vital, but only in the context of the gospel. And the gospel was missing from the package we were offering the world.

At this juncture of Adventist history, God chose two young men to break the bands of legalism in the church by articulating the correct relation between the law and the gospel.

"The Lord in His great mercy sent a most precious message to His people through Elders Waggoner and Jones. This message was to bring more prominently before the world the uplifted Savior, the sacrifice for the sins of the whole world. It presented justification through faith in the Surety; it invited the people to receive the righteousness of Christ, which is made manifest in obedience to all the commandments of God. Many had lost sight of Jesus. They needed to have their eyes directed to His divine person, His merits, and His changeless love for the human family. All power is given into His hands, that He may dispense rich gifts unto men, imparting the priceless gift of His own righteousness to the helpless human agent. This is the message that God commanded to be given to the world. It is the third angel's message, which is to be proclaimed with a loud voice, and attended with the outpouring of His Spirit in a large measure" (*Testimonies to Ministers,* pp. 91, 92).

A.T. Jones and E.J. Waggoner attended the 1888 General Conference session with a message from the Lord. The exact contents of their message at that meeting has been debated by Adventists ever since they delivered it. Whatever we want to say about the message, there are a few things that are absolutely clear as we research the topic in the writings of Ellen White:

1. The message was given to correct a condition of legalism that had become prevalent in the church.

2. It was a message that exalted Christ to a central position of prominence and magnified the completeness of His sacrifice for the sins of the whole world.

3. It was a message of justification by faith in Christ alone, giving absolutely no merit to any works of righteousness that we have done or can do.

4. It was a message that defined the proper function of the law as a mirror to show us our sin and as a schoolmaster to make evident our need of Christ, but never as a means of gaining God's favor or salvation through obedience to its requirements.

5. It was a message that promised to produce obedience and victory as the inevitable fruit of true Biblical faith, which works by love, in

the empowering light of the cross.

Ellen White identified the message of Jones and Waggoner as the beginning of the loud cry and the latter rain. She pleaded with our people to receive the heaven-sent proclamation. If we would, the whole world would soon be lightened with the glory of God and Jesus would return.

Whether that message was accepted or rejected has also been a matter of debate in the church. There are a number of Spirit of Prophecy quotations that clearly indicate that the message was largely rejected. But I feel no need to prove that point with quotations. The very fact that over a hundred years has elapsed since the message was first given is proof enough. If the message had been received, the gospel commission would have been fulfilled long ago.

Rather than embracing the glorious light of the gospel of God's free grace, the church responded to Jones and Waggoner by pulling farther to the right in an effort to defend the law against what was perceived as a liberal trend creeping into the church. Instead of discerning the need for a more Christ-centered message, the church felt threatened by the call to a love-motivated faith alone as the basis for salvation.

Ellen White lamented our deplorable, self-righteous blindness. She devoted the remainder of her life to the painstaking task of trying to steer the church toward Christ and His gospel. Books such as *Steps to Christ, The Desire of Ages, Thoughts from the Mount of Blessing,* as well as numerous *Review* and *Signs* articles reflect that effort on her part.

Finally, she passed off the scene of action.

# The Great Advent Pendulum

Despite her clear written appeals to uplift Jesus, to magnify His pardoning love demonstrated on the cross, the church, by and large, continued in its law-standards-works-doctrine oriented focus. (I emphasize the word focus because, of course, God's law and Bible doctrine must not be cast aside as of little importance, but must not occupy a place of prominence that would compromise the gospel.) Generation after generation of Adventist youth were raised and educated in a vacuum of Christless preaching, Christless worship, and Christless efforts to keep the law. As the desperate decades rolled by, the people in the pews were continually admonished to "get ready" for Jesus to come by striving to overcome sin and attain perfection of character. Evangelistic efforts continued in the tradition of doctrinal defense and largely aimed for intellectual conversions. A liberal backlash was in the making.

Eventually, as is inevitable with pendulum action, pressure began to build on the right. Soon the pendulum would begin its swing left. A gnawing inner sense of need for grace, for mercy, for Jesus, would produce a reactionary leftward movement. When we're too far right to see Jesus, it is necessary to move left in ordered to find balance. But inherent in that quest is the danger of overshooting the mark and moving too far left. And that's exactly what began to happen.

Liberalism was born in Adventism. A few bold and prominent voices began to suggest that certain distinctive Adventist doctrines are contrary to grace. The judgment, obedience, standards, indeed the whole idea of overcoming sin in this life—all was cast aside as hostile to the gospel. Such was the natural scourge that lay restlessly sleeping for over a century in the legalistic heart of Adventism.

The casting off of any teaching that smacks of requirement appeals to the human spirit when it has done time in the prison of futile efforts to live the Christian life without the love of Christ aflame in the soul. For many Seventh-day Adventists the liberal trend in the church has offered a refreshing sensation. Spiritually exhausted by all *the do's and don'ts* of Adventism, and having never understood the how's and why's embodied in the gospel, some have found a false sense of liberty in the daring denials of Bible truth that have emerged among us in recent decades.

And so, Adventism has become an arena in which liberal and conservative factions contend for supremacy. We've seen in recent decades various changes in the church that have been perceived as the result of liberal influences. In response, we've also seen a proliferation of watchman-on-the-wall type ministries that feel it their duty to defend and preserve our conservative past. Everyone with open eyes has witnessed the mounting tension between conservative and liberal influences in the church. Publications, audio and video cassettes are flooding the church from hundreds if not thousands of sources debating numerous issues of doctrine and practice.

- What kind of human nature did Jesus have—fallen or unfallen?

- Is perfection of character necessary or even possible?
- Is there really any such thing as an investigative judgment in a heavenly sanctuary, and is 1844 of any significance?
- Was the atonement complete on the cross?
- What about the nature of man's sin problem— is he guilty by virtue of what he is in the flesh, or only by virtue of his personal deeds of sin?
- Are we saved by grace through faith alone, or do good works play a part in our salvation?
- How inspired is the Spirit of Prophecy, or the Bible for that matter?
- Is health reform really necessary?
- What about dress, jewelry, makeup, mixed swimming, television, competitive sports, drama, rhythmic music, fiction, and other lifestyle issues? What's right and what's wrong?

I'll end the list there so as not to exhaust you. I think you get my point. We're *not* one big happy family at the present moment. The voices are many and divergent. The atmosphere is hot.

As the tension intensifies with conservatives pulling the bungy cord of truth to the right and liberals pulling to the left, what is the next inevitable act in the unfolding drama? Perhaps the cord will break under all the pressure and send each side plunging into total division? Maybe the cord will eventually pull us all back together in unity? It is more likely, however, that both division and unity will occur in our ranks, out of which will emerge two new camps to replace the present conservative-liberal dichotomy.

I'd like to share what I believe will be the crescendo scenario that will break the Adventist stalemate.

Presently we see two basic factions in the church: (1) The conservatives on the right, defending the law, standards, overcoming sin, etc., and (2) the liberals on the left, emphasizing love, acceptance, mercy, etc. Each side views the other as an enemy to truth.

It is natural for us to assume that one group is all right and the other all wrong. The way we project that perception depends, of course, on which camp we best identify with personally. If conservative in our leanings, we will tend to view those more liberal than ourselves as the tares in the church. If liberal in our leanings, then we will tend to view those more conservative than ourselves as the tares. The basic reason for perceiving the situation this way is probably that we all tend to build on one foundational assumption—"I'm right." Consequently, those who agree with me are right also. Everyone else is "off."

While it is natural for us to think this way, it definitely is not right. If we pause before the Lord long enough to get a generous dose of humility, we may begin to see a different picture. A little honest reflection may persuade us that there are both wheat and tares mingled in each camp, even the one we don't particularly care for.

Within the liberal faction of the church there are true-hearted men and women who genuinely love Jesus, and there are those who are at heart world-loving compromisers. The same is true of the conservative faction. Among them there are those who are totally devoted Christian people who love the Lord with all their hearts, and there are those who are governed by self-righteousness and condemnation for others.

Presently we are faced with an illusion far too illusive for any human mind to unravel. The present two factions we see do not represent a clear distinction between the good and the evil. Both camps are a mixture of sheep and goats. It is not as easy as asking whether a person takes a pre-fall or post-fall position on the nature of Christ, or whether he or she is a vegetarian. "Man looks on the outward appearance, but God looks on the heart." The real factor that will ultimately determine who are wheat and who are tares is *spirit,* or *character.*

"As we near the judgment, all will manifest their true character, and it will be made plain to what company they belong" (*Testimonies for the Church,* vol. 1, p. 100).

Apparently, it is not now clear who's who. We cannot presently judge who are the wise and who are the foolish. All present judgment of this magnitude is premature. We must "judge nothing before the time" (1 Corinthians 4:5). Now is the time when characters are forming. Some are cultivating a spirit of condemnation toward others. Some are cultivating a spirit of Christlike love. Eventually, time and test will make it manifest who are in Christ and who are in league with the bitter one who departed heaven with accusations on his lips.

Both division and unity will occur in the church, and two new groups will emerge. All who are partakers of the spirit of Christ, in both the conservative and the liberal camps, will find themselves ultimately united in that spirit. They will have the

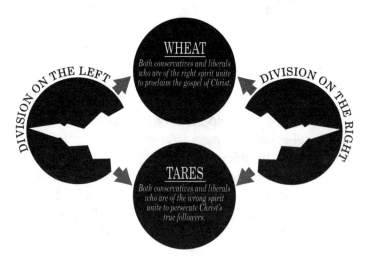

DIVISION ON THE LEFT

DIVISION ON THE RIGHT

WHEAT
*Both conservatives and liberals who are of the right spirit unite to proclaim the gospel of Christ.*

TARES
*Both conservatives and liberals who are of the wrong spirit unite to persecute Christ's true followers.*

# *The Great Advent Pendulum*

Christian courage and humility to lay aside their minor differences and unite on a platform of Christ-centered truth. The true, biblical gospel of the kingdom will dawn in their hearts like the rising of the morning sun. Love and obedience, faith and works, justice and mercy, law and grace will fuse in their experience.

On the other hand, all who are of the spirit of accusation and condemnation, whether conservative or liberal according to present appearances, will find themselves merging together to persecute Christ in the person of His true followers. A common spirit of self-righteousness will unite them.

Stop and think. I mean really think, soberly, transparently, introspectively. Shut out the voices from the right and from the left for a period of serious, personal reflection. Confront yourself with some *stark realities* and ask yourself some *heart-searching questions.*

*Stark Reality:* There will be many people in heaven who didn't have all the right doctrines but had the right spirit. But there will be no one in heaven who had all the right doctrines but cherished the wrong spirit.

*Heart-searching Question:* While I strive to know the whole truth and nothing but the truth, do I also strive to relate with Christlike love and respect to those who do not see all things as I do?

*Stark Reality:* Outward appearances and intellectual beliefs can be self-deceiving. It is possible for a person to practice high standards of righteousness in outward matters, and to profess strong conviction of truths, and yet not truly be in Christ.

*Heart-searching Question:* Is my Christianity heart-level deep? Have I truly, personally encountered the cross and fallen in love with Jesus? Or do I just believe "the truth"?

*Stark Reality:* No matter what I claim to believe, and no matter how careful I am to practice my convictions, if I harbor condemnation in my heart toward any other human being, especially my religious enemies, I am not abiding under the conscious influence of divine forgiveness. The way I feel toward my enemies is the gauge that reveals whether I am partaking of God's pardoning love for me.

*Heart-searching Question:* Do I judge others as God's enemies because I perceive them as enemies to what I believe to be the truth? Do I speak negatively about them or manifest an attitude of disdain for them? Or do I assume they're honest and pray for them?

> *When the last theological argument is argued,*
> *When every heart is finally mature with love*
> *    or hatred,*
> *When the last division divides and the final*
> *    unity unites,*
> *When the great advent pendulum ceases to*
> *    swing,*
> *Where will you . . . and I . . . be standing?*

It is my sincere hope and prayer that we will be found as one in Christ.

# CHAPTER SEVEN

# *Ellen White's "Mistake"*

I'm sure to have gotten your attention with that chapter title. The very thought is enough to make even the healthiest Adventist blood curdle. I can hear some defender of the faith snarling, "Wait just a minute. Ellen White was a prophet. What in the wide world do you mean by using the word mistake in close proximity to her name?"

Before you get your Adventist heart pumping too awfully fast, let me tell you what I mean. Better yet, I'll let her tell you:

"Oh, how I long for Jesus to come, how I long for Him to set things in order. I am now becoming convicted that I have made a mistake in specifying wrongs existing in my brethren. Many are so constituted that they will take these wrongs and deal so severely with the wrong-doer that he will have no courage or hope to set himself right, and this mis-management will ruin a soul. They, knowing the things I know, treat the erring in altogether a different manner than I would. Hereafter I must exercise more caution. I will not trust my brethren to deal with souls, if God will forgive me where I have erred. I plead with all to look away from me, look away from human, finite, erring men's opinions, and look to Jesus. Plead with the dear Lord, talk much less with different ones and pray more . . . I wish that we had much more of the spirit of Christ and a great deal less self and less of human opinions. If we err, let it be on the side of mercy rather than on the side of condemnation and harsh dealing" (Letter #16-1887; partially released in Manuscript Release #449, pp. 28-30).

There it is—Ellen White's "mistake," by her own admission.

Careful now!

Don't let this quotation shake your confidence in her prophetic gift. No, she was not mistaken in her proclamation of the great system of Bible truth so comprehensively embodied in the Advent faith. Nor was she mistaken in the great wealth of practical counsel she delivered to the church. But she did come to regret "specifying wrongs" existing in her brethren.

Why?

Not because her discernment of the wrongs was inaccurate or imaginary. Not because there was no real need for correcting the wrongs she saw. But because "many," not a few, "are so constituted that they will take these wrongs and deal so severely with the wrong-doer that he will have no courage or hope to set himself right, and this mismanagement will ruin a soul."

She didn't regret her efforts to correct the wrongs she saw. She did regret, however, how her more rebuke-oriented statements were used by others. Many would take up her words of correction and use them to deal "severely with the wrongdoer." "Mismanagement" was the word she selected to describe this tragic way of handling of her writings. The words she penned with one spirit were quoted with quite a different spirit. "They [those who mismanage her words], knowing what I know," she grieved, "treat the erring in altogether a different manner than I would." It would seem, then, that the right or wrong management of her writings depends much on the spirit and intent with which they are quoted. According to her own testimony, it is a mismanagement of her writings to administer condemnation to the erring while quoting her for support.

Apparently, Ellen White was so frustrated by this misuse of her writings that she felt personally responsible for the problem, so much so that she confessed it as a mistake on her part and asked the Lord to forgive her. Out of this trying experience, a heaven-born principle crystallized in Ellen's mind: "If we err, let it be on the side of mercy rather than on the side of condemnation and harsh dealing."

She recognized this principle as the true manifestation of "the spirit of Christ" and wished that our people had "much more" of it.

The prophet Micah beautifully articulated this concept as a basic requirement of God:

# Abandon Ship?

"He hath shewed thee, O man, what is good; and what doth the Lord require of thee, but to do justly, and to love mercy, and to walk humbly with thy God?" (Micah 6:8).

I had read and quoted this verse for years before its meaning finally dawned on me. Micah is here expressing the fundamental rule for dealing with one's self and with others.

- The basic rule for dealing with myself is to apply *justice*—"to do justly." God requires me to hold myself accountable to the highest dictates of conscience, to be conservative in my personal accountability to Him.
- But the basic rule for dealing with others is to apply *mercy*—"to love mercy." God requires me to exercise endless and abundant compassion toward others, to be liberal in love, generous in pardon toward those who err.

To live in this way equates to "walking humbly with thy God." But as fallen human beings we tend to be selfish in our perceptions. We find it more natural to apply the strictest standard of justice to others and to be liberal in mercy toward ourselves. To live in this way equates to walking in self-righteousness and pride before the Lord. To condemn another person is, in effect, to claim personal innocence. When we relate to our fellow human beings with an attitude of judgment, we deny our own need of God's forgiveness and demand His acceptance on the basis of our personal righteousness. Of course, there is no such acceptance available, because, in reality, we are each one as guilty as the other guy. The righteousness we think we see in ourselves is merely a self-induced illusion born of condemnation toward others.

It is inevitable—you are going to encounter wrongs in your fellow church members. You will see failure and error in those with whom you share the name of Christ. There will be occasions when you feel it necessary to deal with the wrongs you notice. When you feel a need to do so, there is a serious, heart-searching question I'd like to suggest you ask yourself:

"What is my purpose—to expose and condemn the wrong-doer, or to restore the wrong-doer and cover a multitude of sins."

The motive with which you approach the sensitive matter of correcting others will shape your spirit as you execute the unpleasant task. If it is your objective to win and restore, then there is only one proper and effective approach. Take this counsel to heart:

"The erring can be restored in *no other* way than in the spirit of meekness, gentleness, and tender love" (*Testimonies for the Church,* vol. 2, p. 52; italics supplied).

"No one has ever been reclaimed from a wrong position by censure and reproach; but many have thus been driven from Christ and led to seal their hearts against conviction. A tender spirit, a gentle, winning deportment, may save the erring and hide a multitude of sins. The revelation of Christ in your own character will have a transforming power upon all with whom you come in contact" (*Thoughts from the Mount of Blessing,* pp. 128, 129).

# Abandon Ship?

The same principle applies when dealing with the church as a whole:

"We are not to hurl the thunderbolts against the church of Christ militant; for Satan is doing all he possibly can in this line, and you who claim to be the remnant of the people of God had better not be found helping him, denouncing, accusing, and condemning. Seek to restore, not to tear down, discourage, and destroy" (*Review and Herald,* vol. 6, p. 516).

"Let every one who is seeking to live a Christian life, remember that the church militant is not the church triumphant. Those who are carnally minded will be found in the church. They are to be pitied more than blamed. The church is not to be judged as sustaining these characters, though they be found within her borders. . . . Jesus saw the bad and the good in church relationship, and said, 'Let both grow together until the harvest'" (*Fundamentals of Christian Education,* pp. 294, 295).

"The Lord wants His people to follow other methods than that of condemning wrong, even though the condemnation be just. He wants us to do something more than to hurl at our adversaries charges that only drive them further from the truth. The work which Christ came to do in our world was not to erect barriers and constantly thrust upon the people the fact that they were wrong.

"He who expects to enlighten a deceived people must come near to them and labor for them in love. He must become a center of holy influence" (*Testimonies for the Church,* vol. 6, pp. 121, 122).

If these quotations don't seem strikingly appropriate for our time, then rejoice that you are not on the wrong mailing lists. Ours is a time when condemnation has been mastered as a fine art under the pretense of defending truth. The church is presently faced with an entire movement that resides on the edges of Adventism specializing in exposing and condemning wrong. Some consider themselves professional rebukers. From a financial standpoint, it really can be quite a lucrative profession. As one shrewd master of the trade confessed with tongue in cheek to a group of fellow rebukers, "When I expose error and rebuke the church, the money really comes in. But when I've tried just preaching the gospel, funds decreased."

Now I know how some folks will respond to the ideas put forth in this chapter. Whenever I share these things someone is always quick to balance me out:

"Yes, what you're saying is true . . . for some people, but we're not all alike, and we're not all called to the same kind of ministry. Some of us just tell it like it is and let the chips fall where they may. Some of us are just not gentle. We speak straight, and if you can't bear it, that's your problem. Some of us are like Elijah, John the Baptist and the Protestant Reformers."

I must confess, I've never liked the paintings of John the Baptist that portray him with matted hair and furrowed eyebrows, gritting his teeth with an outstretched arm and pointed finger. In all honesty, I'm glad nothing in the Bible tells us that religious art is inspired by the Holy Spirit. Scripture records only the words of John; we add the tone, the look, the attitude we imagine he possessed. The same is true of Elijah. And as far as the reformers are concerned, Ellen White had this to say:

"Men who are harsh and censorious often excuse or try to justify their lack of Christian politeness because some of the Reformers worked with such a spirit, and they claim that the work for this time requires the same spirit; but this is not so. A spirit which is calm and under perfect control is better in any place, even in the roughest company. A furious zeal does no good to anyone. God did not select the Reformers because they were overbearing, passionate men. He accepted them as they were, notwithstanding these traits of character; but He would have placed tenfold greater responsibilities upon them had they been of humble mind, having their spirits under control of reason" (*Testimonies for the Church,* vol. 4, p. 486).

If Ellen White herself, a woman endowed with the prophetic gift, regretted "specifying wrongs" that she saw in her brethren, how can we not sense the need to be extremely careful in our dealing with those who err. And if she was frustrated over the mismanagement of her writings to deal harshly with wrong-doers, how can we not exercise great caution in our use of her words today.

It is my prayer that we will determine to live by the rule she settled on: "If we err, let it be on the side of mercy rather than on the side of condemnation and harsh dealing."

# CHAPTER EIGHT

# The Liberal Conservative

I want to tell you about a man who confused everyone. Oh, he didn't mean to, but he did. No one could figure him out.

Conservative? Yes . . . well, no . . . well, maybe, maybe not.

Liberal? It would seem so. Well, maybe not. Oh, certainly he was. On second thought, no.

See what I mean? He put everyone into a tizzy of frustration trying to figure out where he stood.

After a while he became the talk of the town, especially among church folks. At first they seemed amused by his apparent fickleness, but soon they got downright mad at him.

"Would you please quit being so wishy-washy and join one camp or the other," someone finally voiced the tension everyone seemed to feel.

After watching him carefully for some time, one

of the town's people noticed a consistent pattern to his behavior.

"Yes, yes, there is definitely rhyme and reason to this guy's life," the man tried to explain to his friends and neighbors.

They just scoffed at him: "No way! We hope you don't end up as confused as he is. You had better stop watching him so closely."

"But there really is a consistent pattern," he mumbled to himself as the people walked away.

"I've been watching him carefully," he continued reasoning with himself. "With regards to his own relationship with God, he is very conservative. He is consistent in prayer. He is jealous for the truth of God's word. He is temperate in his lifestyle, conscientious in his labors, and serious in his manner. But when it comes to the failings of others, he is extremely liberal. While others condemn, he defends and forgives those who do wrong. He is conservative to apply justice to himself, yet liberal in exercising mercy toward others. Conservative in personal obedience to God's word, but liberal in forgiving those who fail to do the same.

"Yes, I'm sure of it. There is a consistent pattern to his life. Why can't anyone see it. He's really not a bad guy. Actually, I think we would all be better off if we were like HIM."

Before too long, the town's people got so angry at his conservative-liberal ways that they crucified Him.

---

According to the conservative Pharisees, Jesus

was far too liberal for their liking. They were in the habit of condemning sinners. He was in the habit of forgiving them. They were in the habit of lifting their noses to the outcasts of society, and no doubt holding their self-righteous breath as they hurried by so as not to inhale any tainted air. He was in the habit of dining with the outcasts and putting an affirming hand on their shoulders. They were in the habit of pronouncing curses on all who were not of their mold. He was in the habit of pronouncing blessings on everyone . . . except those who were in the habit of pronouncing curses.

He didn't fit in with the liberal Sadducees either. They had little respect for the Scriptures, except when some passage could be used to their political advantage. He quoted the Scriptures continually and exalted every word as God-inspired. They loved to be served by the more common folks. He loved to serve the more common folks. They grasped for wealth and power. He possessed none of this world's wealth or power, and wanted none.

The Pharisees and Sadducees were on opposite ends of the religious spectrum—the Pharisees to the far right and the Sadducees to the far left. So, of course, they didn't get along too well. They were in constant contention over theological and lifestyle issues.

However, they did have one important thing in common—they hated each other. So in a round about way they were of the same spirit. That's why it was natural for them to unite against Jesus. They saw in Him what both of their camps lacked—the perfect balance of hatred for sin and love for sinners.

## Abandon Ship?

For them, it was the other way around—they hated sinners, but secretly loved sin.

Deep inside, they knew He was all that they should be. But the bad combination of pride and secret sin made it necessary for them to put Him to death along with their conscience.

Are you listening?

## CHAPTER NINE
# *The Spirit's Whisper*

Shhhh. Be quiet . . .

That's not meant to be a polite way of saying "shut up." I mean what David meant with his frequent use of *Selah* throughout the Psalms.

*Pause.*

*Stop.*

*Listen.*

For what?

For the deeper meaning. For the more unfeigned sense of truth. For the truer balance. For the voice of God.

And that's not such an easy task these days. There are so many voices clamoring for attention. You've heard them. Some call from the right—to holiness, to obedience, to high standards. Some call from the left—to faith, to love, to mercy. Some say what matters is how you live your life. Some say what matters is that you accept others regardless of how they live their lives.

What does really matter . . . to God?

As your head follows your ears to the right and then to the left, there is another voice. A third call. It is not so loud as the others. But it is more fervent. This voice seems only a whisper in the background of a shouting match, but more powerful still.

A whisper—not because it's weak, but because it's only meant to be heard by those who will be quiet and listen.

What does the voice say as it whispers?

Does it add its invitation to the strident challenges to overcome sin that come from the right? Or does it echo the plea for mercy that we hear on the left?

Be quiet . . . and listen . . . to the whisper:

"And thine ears shall hear a word behind thee, saying, This is the way, walk ye in it, when ye turn to the right hand, and when ye turn to the left" (Isaiah 30:21).

"Ye shall not turn aside to the right hand or to the left" (Deuteronomy 5:32).

Don't go to the right, says the voice, and don't go to the left. Walk straight forward. Don't emphasize justice to the exclusion or minimizing of mercy, and don't emphasize mercy to the exclusion or minimizing of justice. Don't get so hung up on obedience to My law that you fail to abide in My love, and don't get so focused on love that you miss the importance of obedience.

This voice beckons us to

- A love *that does* obey (see John 14:15).
- A grace *that does* transform (see Titus 2:11-16).
- A faith *that does* work (see Galatians 5:5, 6).
- A forgiveness *that does* empower (see John 8:8-11).

Listen to the voice carefully. It does not merely command us to obey, as do the voices to the far right. Nor does it merely seek to stimulate our emotions with sentimental love, as we hear from the far left.

No, no, no!

This voice is so unique that it's unmistakable. The Spirit whispers of a love that does, by virtue of its own power, create in us a heart that obeys the will of God, *for the sake of love.* The Spirit's whisper will not be heard urging righteous living as a means to attain any degree of acceptance with God. For "by the deeds of the law there shall no flesh be justified in His sight" (Romans 3:20). The Pharisees "also outwardly appear righteous" (Matthew 23:28). Nor will the voice of the Spirit be heard offering a faith that replaces the need for works. "The devils also believe, and tremble. . . . Faith without works is dead" (James 2:19, 20).

No demands for heartless reform that leave the soul void of any deep sense of divine love, and no offer of cheap grace that gives license to sin, is to be found in the sure word of the whispering One. Rather, He promises an abounding, all sufficient grace—so free, so accepting, so absolutely unmerited, that all who truly perceive and receive it *will be* changed by that very grace, *because of grace.*

# Abandon Ship?

That voice—that whispering, faithful voice—was once heard through a man, THE MAN. When He walked the earth there were some, like there are today, who dealt with sin by excusing the sinner. There were others, as there are now, who dealt with sin by condemning the sinner. But not this Man. Healing the sin problem at both levels, conquering its guilt and its power, Jesus offered a forgiveness so full and free that all who received it were also made victorious by it. To the woman caught in adultery He proclaimed His gospel for all: "Neither do I condemn thee: go and sin no more" (John 8:11).

I do not condemn you, whoever you are, whatever you've done.

I do not condemn you, before you do good, before you even desire to do good.

I do not condemn you, not because you deserve My mercy, but because I love you.

Now then, in the light of My love, in the healing embrace of My forgiveness, under the empowering motivation of My grace, go and sin no more.

We all sense in our experience a degree of fluctuation as we hear voices from the right and from the left. When a preacher on the right exhorts the church to good works and holy living, our hearts say, "Yes, I really should be more conscientious." When a preacher on the left expounds God's great mercy, again our hearts respond, "Yes, that's what I need to hear." But there is no need for confusion. Hold fast to that which is good. The Lord is not asking you to choose between

- Law and grace
- Love and obedience
- Forgiveness or victory
- Faith and works

The Christian journey is somewhat like a tightrope walk. As you put one foot in front of the other, you may start to lean too far right or left. In your hands is the balancing rod, the word of God. The weight on the right is the law. The weight on the left is God's offer of mercy. As you begin to tip right, the balancing rod tips left to remind you of the Lord's great pardoning love. As you begin to tip left, the balancing rod tips right to remind you that true love leads to obedience.

The law has a function: To show us our sin and arouse our sense of need for grace. That's all. The law does its job well when we allow it this role. But when we hold up the law and start requiring obedience as a solution to the sin problem, we take the law beyond its intended purpose and set ourselves up for self-righteousness or despair.

Grace has its function: To release us from the condemnation of the law by revealing God's loving forgiveness. In turn, the realization of that love arouses in us a grateful, affectionate faith that produces burden-free obedience. Grace does its job well when we allow it to abound in our preaching and in our relating to others. But when grace is offered as a release from the law's legitimate requirements, then grace is distorted and can only lead to hypocrisy or immorality.

Grace informs us that God's love is greater than

the law's condemnation, so much greater that it compelled Him to sacrifice Himself, in the person of His Son, to effect full and free forgiveness for us. The pardon is given by virtue of His goodness, not in response to our obedience. Obedience is not the Savior. Jesus is the Savior, who, by His saving grace, wins our hearts to eager obedience.

This is the voice I have heard as I've paused to listen. Perhaps its the voice you've been hearing as well. If not, I'd like to ask that you be quiet for awhile. Shut out every other voice. Open your Bible with a new prayer for understanding. And listen.

I think you'll find that "When every other voice is hushed, and in quietness we wait before Him, the silence of the soul makes more distinct the voice of God" (*The Ministry of Healing,* p. 58).

Shhhh.